If My Cherry Could Talk

If My Cherry Could Talk

A POETIC COLLECTION OF TASTY EROTICA

*To Daddy Love,
Celebrate Sexually
truly,
CURV
22 Jan 17*

CREATED BY

Curv BROWN

Sugar Sweet Love, LLC
www.sugarsweetlove.com

Sugar Sweet Love, LLC
www.sugarsweetlove.com

This is a work of fiction. Names, characters, businesses, places, and events are either the products of the author's imagination or are used in a fictitious manner. Any resemblance to actual persons, living or dead, or actual events is purely coincidental.

Copyright © 2016 by Curv Brown

All rights reserved. No part of this book may be reproduced or transmitted in any form or by any means, electronic or mechanical, including photocopying, recording, or any information storage and retrieval system, without permission in writing from Curv Brown.

ISBN: 978-0-9965301-0-1

10 9 8 7 6 5 4 3 2   1 2 2 2 1 5

Printed in the United States of America

Artwork by Curv Brown
Cover painting: My Cherry Talks
Photos by Hollins Photography

♾This paper meets the requirements of ANSI/NISO Z39.48-1992 (Permanence of Paper)

Dedication

This assortment of seduction

is dedicated

to the women

who first encouraged me

to be myself

and live free

Sugar and Mommie

{ my extraordinary grandmothers }

who lovingly nurtured

my uniqueness

plus

my Beautiful mother

who patiently transferred

my journal entries

from scribble to script

Sex

without

Love

is

as

hollow

&

ridiculous

as

Love

without

Sex

~

Hunter S. Thompson

(writer, journalist)

Contents

Acknowledgments	💋	xiii
My Missionary Position	💋	xv
Introduction	💋	xvii
Painting: The Verbal Vagina	💋	xx
Invitation	💋	xxi

Chapter 1   1

POPPERS
Platinum Orgasm Producers

Painting: Cherry's Chocolate	♥	2
Verbally	♥	3
Filthy 5-Letter Favorites: CREAM	♥	6
Brand New Way	♥	7
The Dick Wish	♥	8
Quoteworthy: Good Wood	♥	11
Phone Freak:		
{Coming} / Blue Light Special	♥	12
{Going} / What Cha Doing	♥	13
Quoteworthy: Life or Death	♥	16
Her Hardworking Man	♥	17
Orgasmic Deviations	♥	18
Trouple: 3 Intimately	♥	20
ON	♥	22
Six Senses {Smell}: scented	♥	24
INTOXICATED	♥	25

My Body's Soul Mate	♥	26
The Lesson	♥	28
fresh peaches	♥	30
Curv Cummentary: Better Blow	♥	31
genital giant	♥	34
Why Is It Just An Annual	♥	36
The Man In Me: Kitty Passion	♥	41
Oral Orgasm	♥	42
Sugar Smacks	♥	44
Hard Ship	♥	45
Filthy 5-Letter Favorites: ERECT	♥	46
Piece-Taker	♥	47
vicious	♥	48
Quoteworthy: Lust vs. Love	♥	50
Quoteworthy: Laughter	♥	51
Pop Cum Snow	♥	52
Supreme Beam (Part I)	♥	54
Supreme Beam (Part II)	♥	55
Glossary of Genitalia: Vagina	♥	58
Glossary of Genitalia: Penis	♥	59

Chapter 2   61

Deliciously Wicked
When Naughty Meets Nasty

Painting: Jezebel DeVine	♥	62
Ain't Gon Make It	♥	63
Quoteworthy: Music	♥	66

Spin Cycle {½ poem}	♥	67
Share Your Shit	♥	68
hard lay on a hard day	♥	72
3rd Glass of Wine	♥	74
Misbehave Soundwave:		
which tone turns you on?	♥	76
STEAM	♥	78
Anything Like Me	♥	80
freak's bizarre	♥	83
Six Senses {Taste}: a sample	♥	83
Ya Damn Right	♥	84
Do You Know…THE BASES	♥	88
Meek the Freak	♥	89
Instead	♥	90
Filthy 5-Letter Favorites: TAINT	♥	93
teetering	♥	94
Wishful Thinking	♥	96
Our Founding Fuckers: Vanessa and Alfred	♥	97
Interview With A Master	♥	98
Sadistic Star	♥	101
The Man In Me: Holding Me	♥	102
Curv Cummentary: Every Bootie		
does not belong in pornography	♥	104
Veteran Vanity	♥	108
How I Like It	♥	110
They All Want To See	♥	112
Six Senses {See}: whom shall he love	♥	113
fantasy #8 {½ poem}	♥	114

Can't Help Himself	♥	115
She Winks, He Smiles	♥	116
Sap Drunk Love	♥	118
Jurassic	♥	119
Backstage Pass	♥	121
Quoteworthy: Pleasure's Price	♥	122
Filthy 5-Letter Favorites: PUSSY	♥	123
Curv Cummentary: The Benefits of a Small Dick	♥	124

Chapter 3 — 127

Screw-Arounds & Let-Downs
Cheating Lovers / Sorry Fuckers

Painting: Corrosive	♥	128
i love you too much to...	♥	129
The P Word	♥	130
Puppy In The Window	♥	132
Filthy 5-Letter Favorites: TRAIN	♥	134
2ndman (Part I)	♥	135
2ndman (Part II)	♥	136
Quoteworthy: Trickery	♥	137
Quickie Questionnaire: Pornographic Preoccupations	♥	138
RESERVED	♥	142
Goodbye, Goldie	♥	144

Quoteworthy: Size	♥	147
your boo left her boo-hooing	♥	148
Filthy 5-Letter Favorites:		
FREAK VS. WHORE	♥	149
Snake In My Grass	♥	150
He Called Today	♥	152
Curv Cummentary:		
Porn has Purpose	♥	154
I'll Lease Your Man	♥	158
Passing Plastic	♥	160
Six Senses {Hear}: one word	♥	161
The Business Transaction	♥	162
Shit and You	♥	164
Predator	♥	167
DICKTIONARY	♥	168

Chapter 4   171
Southern Comfort
Threesomes with Me, Myself, & I

Painting: Sarong on Sea Breeze	♥	172
Monkey's Demands	♥	173
Quickie Questionnaire:		
Speak To Your Freak	♥	176
Six Senses {ESP}:		
Claire's Voyance	♥	178
Quoteworthy: The Unknown	♥	179
Piping Hot	♥	180

The Man In Me: Mentally	♥	182
Filthy 5-Letter Favorites: DILDO	♥	184
Her Little Black Dildo	♥	185
The Man In Me: Girl of my Dreams	♥	186
Fucking for One: Masturbational Matching	♥	187
Sticky Fingers	♥	188
Quoteworthy: Education	♥	193
Do you know…The Sex Holidays	♥	194
Freaky Aphrodisiacs	♥	195
Curv Cummentary: Recommendation For Masturbation	♥	196
Keep Touching Me	♥	199
Bed Besieged By Brothers	♥	200
Warm Honey Awaits You	♥	202
Nutless	♥	204
Six Senses {Touch}: doing herself	♥	204
Two One-Night Stands	♥	206
Sight Unseen	♥	208
Bona Fide Sex	♥	210
Curv Cummentary: Good Vibrations: Purchasing the Perfect Penis	♥	212
Stimulating Websites	♥	216
The Money Shot	♥	219

Recommended Reading	👄	221
Painting: Showtime	👄	223
About the Author	👄	223
Sales / Shows	👄	225

ACKNOWLEDGMENTS

I first acknowledge my Creator.
Thank you for the Spirit allowing Your artistry
to manifest through me.

Next, I give my deepest gratitude
to my loving family members,
unforgettable ancestors,
and all of my parents, especially my Grands,
Sweet Papa and Sugar.

Your affection and open conversations
kept me from seeking acceptance
in the arms of strangers.
I love you beyond the limitations of words.

Much appreciation to my colorful collection
of wonderful friends
(my sisters and brothers from another mother).
You know who you are.
Your support has sustained me.

Special gratitude goes to
my radiant Diamond,
Stephi, 'Nita, Angie, Mams, Inez, Mera,
and my proofreader, Val.

To everyone who has cheered me on
from the first poem
to the latest and greatest.
I am eternally indebted
for your encouragement.

The light of God surrounds you all.

MY MISSIONARY POSITION

I AM
held responsible for the use
of my God-granted creativity

when this head grows cold
my mind shall rest in peace
knowing I was brave enough
to share my talents
with the multitudes

I was born to write
and encourage a thriving love for self

I was created to speak
and give someone the confidence
to share that loving with others

I AM
here to inspire adults
to participate freely and safely
in consensual sex

let my words
urge somebody
to relax
to laugh
to love
to fuck
RESPONSIBLY

I am truly,

Curv Brown

Introduction

why did I write this book?

Because I am nasty. Honestly, I am.

There are periods in my life when I have been a filthy-minded woman. Maybe this is due to extended periods of dick deprivation. Perhaps masturbation became so routine that writing was an outlet to the built-up frustration of unpredictable sex. But honestly, I enjoy the subject.

Sex is constantly on my mind. I see sex everywhere. Even in my fruits and vegetables. Oranges and peaches are grouped in sets of similar size. Bananas are always thick and/or long. Butternut squash and zucchini are never purchased. Yet, I am forced to take a few seconds and admire them.

when did the writing begin?

I wrote my first poem in 1992, working at a call center with grown folks and privileged part-time college students. There was a tall blond fellow who complained about writing a poem for a class. I said, "Anybody can write a poem." On the spot, I whipped out a sheet of paper and constructed my first. Now this gift of writing has blended with my passionate preoccupation producing this sexually-charged poetry for your enjoyment.

why is it so easy for me to share?

Sex is essential. It is the gateway for humanity. So often we are informed of the dangers versus its beauty and relief. But

I desire to expand discussion of all areas of this multi-faceted topic.

I've always viewed sex a bit differently. From an early age, the thought of it has been a ceaseless, amusing fascination; and it is all good as long as there's sensibility and precaution.

My disposition to sexual thinking might have started during an unforgettable summer in the late seventies. I was friends with the children next door to my grandparents. Unbeknownst to my Grands, their neighbors had an incredible porn collection. I'd go over to play and finger through stacks of magazines. There was *Playboy*, *Hustler*, and bunches of glossy books featuring various races and bodies in baffling positions of physical fulfillment.

could weeks spent goggling over nude women and folks fucking have swayed my mentality?

I don't believe this pictorial exposure to the physical side of sex damaged my psyche. After all, it was a single summer spent playing in a porn paradise. There are so many other events that have had a greater influence on my intimate life. Maybe this one allowed for an early state of open-mindedness. Perhaps this premature experience made me nonchalant about the communication of sexual matters. If anything, it added a comfort that many people don't possess. Today, decades later, sex still hovers in the recesses of my mind. Only now, I choose to allow its expression to flow through me and be shared with others.

exposure. experience. expression.

Sex is a beautiful thing, a prerequisite for life. So how can it be labeled as anything short of miraculous? Without sex, you wouldn't be alive and reading this book. So I ask…isn't satisfying and consensual sex an experience worth writing about?

These pages just hold a few of the bricks needed to pave my destiny. I am a mere messenger who encourages, and sometimes insists on, mature adults releasing inhibitions and being free sexually. But my God-granted gift can't be fully explained because this is simply who I was born to be.

My book is based on our human commonality for seeking pleasure.

This is my mission's manifestation and a universal pleaser. These pages document the countless fortes of physical love from masturbation and lust to soft-sex and fucking.

May my writings stimulate every woman, man, race, and partner preference to become and remain open-minded about the occasional dreadful yet forever beautiful sides of sex.

the curve
IS MORE POWERFUL THAN
the sword

~

Mae West
(actress, playwright)

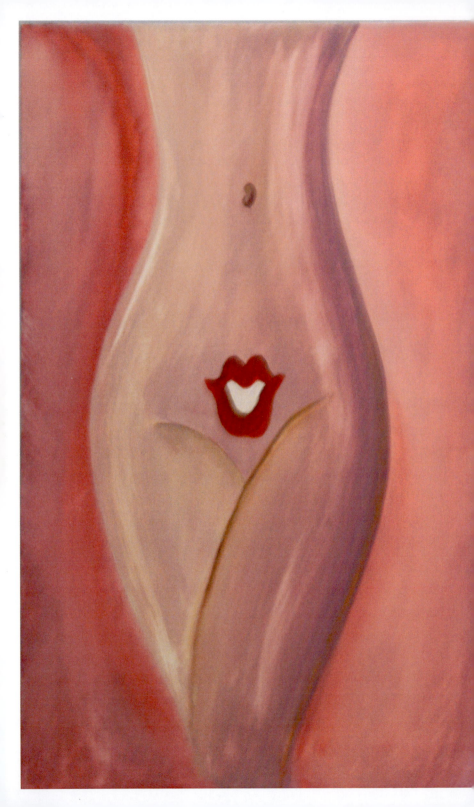

INVITATION

greetings

welcome to my world

in these pages
you'll meet pieces of the real me
and a chunk of my imaginary

as I share myself
from southern lady to high class trick
I invite you to thank your genitals
pussy or dick

open your mind
to what you consider good
causing your cream to churn
turning your softness to wood

think of the things you love
about loving

what makes you harder
what makes you wetter
I invite you
to get to know your freak better

Chapter 1

POPPERS

Platinum Orgasm Producers

VERBALLY

he fed the constant cravings
     of my starving sensuality
       didn't have to guess what
              he thought of me sexually

the man was a talker
found fascination in the formation
     of fragmented sentences
       that sung praises
            to his astounding erotic ability

the type of gentleman
       who always brought
           a cool drink to bed
    guaranteeing
       I heard every word he said

but he was also a wicked man of verbal wizardry

calling me on my job
     just to ask if my ass
       had any idea what's going to happen to it
                later that day
so it was easy letting him and his words
              just have their way

you see, a grandstander was he
     taking possession of my punany's pedestal
       striking seductive poses of flexibility
     as I laid fucked up and frozen
       in the shadows of his sexual shivery

    oh how incessantly
he'd plunge his smoking barrel
     into the depths of my raging sea
             and too happy was me
     for he was my captain
        and I, his first matey

        having my ocean's floor
              displaced by the thrills of his ecstasy
     as he composed yet another rhapsody
           while fucking me oh-so-arrogantly

     because he was
            a wicked man of verbal wizardry

he would get me all tied up and tangled in bed
    and then he'd start fucking with my head
    saying shit like
    "open your eyes...open your eyes
          and look up at me
                while I'm dicking you down"
so I hope you can understand
how I miss having him and that mouthpiece
                      around

verbally
    he'd prep my openness
                for his continual attack
    whispering warnings of his mission
        to generate sweat
             in the center of my back
        to make my tongue
             forget how to speak
        to leave my body
            happy limp wet and weak
        beneath the supremacy
             of his muscular physique

you see, a hotdogger was he
    using his plump wiener
        to muster up extra energy
            for endless lovemaking
catching up my coochie
    on current editions of the karma sutra
    for he carried a weighed bat
        knocking his balls
        into the bleachers
            of my honey bun booty

he treated my fulfillment
                         as a privilege and a duty
      as I laid fucked up and frozen
            in the shadows of his sexual shivery

I would be oh-so-responsive
                    to the dick he laid on me
as my apple bottom
          was caramelized into a candy sweet
as he gritted his teeth
     while pressing his chest
                into the souls of my feet
for he diligently laid pipe
      until a skillful plumber was all I could see

and
I could have listened
       to him talk that talk
                through the years
I longed for him
      to pamper my body
           while setting fires in my ears
and some days
I find myself wishing
     he was still by my side
     happily instructing me
       through the receipt
      of his pillow-top push-ups

leaving me smoking and steaming
      in the breezes of his verbal victory
            'cause a talker was he

and sometimes
      I find myself missing his creativity

there are days when I miss
the many sexy clever ways
         he used to fuck me verbally

Filthy 5-Letter Favorites: CREAM

threatening to withdraw his stirring stick
unless she do as told
a submissive servant by nature is she
and tonight he has taken total control

no debate—her lover could do as he feels
down for whatever—voluntary victim for his thrill
no problem accommodating his will
besides his dick is well-known, tested, and real

tonight as he etches new erotic text
into the passion pits of her hips
he will allow only two words to escape
the panting of her parted lips

and this rule, she must obey
tonight all she can say...is

Yes, Daddy

super-kinky, she must admit
so sexually fulfilling and she loves it

with assertive arrogance in the palm of hand
a slap of her ass reinforces his superior stance

promptly she places her fingers upon his tool
instantly starts sucking out of gratitude
he pulls her hair, as her mouth gets sticky
whispering "oh one more thing, my juicy Nikki
I need to hear you scream
every time I make you cream"

BRAND NEW WAY

lover man
she shall whisper her wish
      for a change of venue
           in the menu
               of your upcoming sex session

tonight
      she wants something spicy
tonight
      she wants more seduction
tonight
      she wants control

and
she shall mount your face
         placing her ass
             upon your chinny chin-chin

she shall look down and see
your mouth covered in cunt
         your chin buried in booty

she'll watch your expressions change
         even though
            she can't see your lips moving

     with a long-awaited squat
she'll settle down
      on your tongue's throne
         until seventh heaven shines
             its goodness upon her face
      and she can reward you
         (her faithful servant)
         with the crème of her queendom
tonight
      she will view you
      from another angle as you taste her
              in a brand new way

THE DICK WISH

we met the other day
our worlds collided
        at an unexpected intersection

we greeted each other
with a questful curiosity
        like two young loins
           sniffing the breeze for pheromones
our paws pouncing
the desert's powder
        as we made circles in the sand
and
the whole time
    while you were scanning
        the width of my hips
        the imprint of my tips
        the plush accommodations of my lips
the whole time
    while you were reviewing me physically
        I was simply thinking about your dick

I was wondering how your back moves
    when your joystick is in control

I was envisioning my hands
    holding to the broadness
        of your shoulders' expansion
        as you blessed me with your rod
                repeatedly

oh yeah
I know you had other thoughts

you wanted to know
if my home would be as accommodating
            as my body
you wanted to know
if my clothes were hung

if my bed was made
if my kitchen was clean

because you were wishing
    I could cook a good meal
        every other Sunday

and you were hoping
    I enjoyed having sex
        every other day

    but you were wondering
    oh yeah, you were really wondering
if I would be willing
    to fully service that dick
        every other, other, other day
            (at the very least)

your undressing eyes
    disclosed some of the things
        you wanted to do to my body
    but
if you would have stopped
    drooling long enough
        to look deep into mine
        you would have known that
            every thought
            I had about you
                somehow, someway
    by side street, expressway, or avenue
        every thought
        I had about you
            led back to your dick

    so while you were blatantly lusting
        repositioning my body
            to match your *Joy of Sex* playing cards
I was bargaining

I was placing bets with Lady Luck
    and planting seeds for Mother Earth

      so under the confinement
      of your stripping stare
my mind's eye
      was closed tightly
           for a hand-clutching
           side-swaying prayer
'cause
I was silently wishing
      and feverishly hoping
           that your dick be good

that was the first prayer
      I ever said for you
           that was my dick wish 💋

Publishing
a sophisticated men's magazine
seemed to me
the best possible way
of fulfilling a dream
I'd been nurturing
ever since I was a teenager:
TO GET LAID A LOT.

~

Hugh Hefner
(founder of Playboy Enterprises, philanthropist)

Quoteworthy:
Good Wood

I have a girl whose pussy is <u>so</u> good,
if you threw it up in the air,
it would turn into

sunshine

~

**Vera, a madam
(Della Reese)**
(minister, actress, singer)
movie: Harlem Nights (1989)

my prick loves you

and when I'm finished,

you're going to love my prick

~

**Algon
(Richard Bolla)**
(adult film and movie actor)
The Satisfiers of Alpha Blue, 1972

☎ **Phone Freak: Coming** ☎

BLUE LIGHT SPECIAL

her call broke the highway's hypnosis

his cell phone's blue neon
    flooded the car's cabin
        shattering his mindless thinking

seeing her name in lights
instantly made his nipples erect

aloud he pled with himself
    not to answer too swiftly
    not to act desperate
    not to jump at her first request
        to see him

he had to fan his flames
    asking his cock to calm down
    hoping it would permit his cognitive side
        to lead the call

in his usual fashion
he awaited the third ring
    cleared his throat
    suck-washed his tongue
    pressed the Send button
        letting the boisterous bluesy tone
            greet her first
        before lowering the volume
            and whispered a hearty "hello"
    then he
tightened his grip on the wheel
pressed her lips closer to his heated ear
stopped breathing and anxiously waited
    for her words to start
        sucking his nipples through the phone 👄

 **Phone Freak: Going**

WHAT CHA DOING

you ventured from the familiar
overridden by a need to freak

horny your ideas
fired upon the bull's eye
of blazing fulfillment

landing in the mist of exhausted momentum

the remedy appeared

his number registered rapidly
"hello."   "hello?"
"hey, I was thinking…"
                    "do I need to pull over…?"

no words, only a soft wind
drifting from your moaning lips
                    caught the line leading to his ear
                    and sped into both of his heads
                    with urgent delivery

                    "what are you doing … now?"
"I'm needing you."
                    "I need to turn around?"
"no…oooh…no."

the phone was shifted
as new dimensions were discovered
you were pushing buttons
dust-covered before he came into your life

                    he imagined
        the rise and fall of your heaving breasts

        the division of your crème-filled thighs

          he imagined the air lassoing your chest
                pulling you back in the mattress
        only to release, letting you rise once more
                      to a new helium high
             knowing you he knew your upper back
                      was brushing the sheet
                with its characteristic curvature
             all effort directed to your clitoris

                        he knew how you loved
                         he knew how you liked it
                he knew how you looked in ecstasy

you knew what he craved
you knew what he liked to feel
you knew what he visualized of you

your knees battled elbows colliding transversely

              as his penis lightly tapped the steering wheel
                          the leather reminded him
                       of your physical playgrounds
                         he thought of slapped skin
                          wiggle, shake, backlash
               the jiggle and shifting of your sweet ass

             contemplating each other's pleasure
                   heightened your senses
              as nerve endings stood on the edge
                of blushing flesh and stiff boners

your speechless tongue
was wetting his distant ear

                         he swore passing cars could hear
                              even with the windows up
                   this had to vibrate and please another

                       he couldn't be the only blessed man
                                on earth at this moment

maybe a phone technician
was checking neighborhood lines
maybe he was standing in that green box
on the side of the road
a little longer than normally required
maybe he was touching himself
envisioning a tap at your door
volunteering his assistance

but driving mesmerized
as your massive movements abound
he knew this didn't stop with him

"tell me when you cum"

his stiffness gained upper momentum
reaching for the breeze blowing
through the open sun roof

except for the move of your hand
and the kiss of your vagina
you were motionless nearing the ultimate sensation

hastening blood to key locations
nipples hard as pebbles
you whispered
"oh baby, I wish you were here...
   because I'm cumMMming"

deeper breaths
and moans held a melodic tone
vibrating your diaphragm

                                         leaving him breathless

your final deflations
slowly sinking and shivering
into satin sheets
              as he envisioned your head tilting back
                    the C in your spine
                softening from lower to upper case

Quoteworthy:
Life or Death

> Sex lies at the root of life,
> and we can never learn to reverence life
> until we know how to understand sex
>
> ~ **Havelock Ellis**
> (English sexual psychologist, physician, social reformer)

Sex is.
There is nothing more to be done about it.
Sex builds no roads, writes no novels
and sex certainly gives
no meaning to anything in life.
But itself.

~ **Gore Vidal**
(writer of essays and Broadway plays)

> **of the delights of this world**
> **man cares most for**
> **sexual intercourse**
> **yet**
> **he has left it**
> **out of his heaven**
>
> ~ **Mark Twain**
> (humorist, Southern author)

Her Hardworking Man

he's working harder to keep her

diamond dazzled fingers & pedicures
garaged leather seats & sunroofs
custom drapes & matching duvets

his family complains
    he's all about money now
    acts like she can't live with less
    she won't suffer a day
        as long as he is breathing

friends lonely
    he used to be there, sitting at the bar
    shooting shit over beers growing warm
        in palms hesitate to go home
        preferring conversations
            about the good old times
            and great old fucks

coworkers grateful (or envious)
    you know he got that side gig
    needs to stop living above means
    always ready to snatch up all the money
    why don't they send him the OT memo
        and tell us if he's busy

none feel the cushion of her cleavage
    nor smell her floral fresh hair
none swim the pools of her eyes
    nor drown in her derriere
none know his bona fide reason
    for treating her as his queen
    'cause who would believe
    she has this sinister sucking, swallowing thing

an orally habitual addiction to his dick
    can't stop, won't stop putting her mouth on it
        so he works hard to keep her happy 👄

ORGASMIC DEVIATIONS

her friends speak of
sheer curtains blowing
      on an ocean breeze in the Caribbean
butterflies floating
      in the fragrance of new blossoms
dreamy fantasies
      with handsome men
           in luxurious places they finance
sandy white beaches at dawn
      accompanying white-wine-enhanced
           visions of the setting sun

so she's left feeling abnormal for
her symphony consists strictly of percussion
her waves rise from an angry sea
      and clash into granite walls
        causing tremors that cleanse coral
           on the deepest ocean's floor

she hears
      screaming tennis balls and cracking bats
      a rooster's crow and an elephant's roar

she sees
      puffing smoke stacks
      grinding wheels of old-fashioned trains
      whips reddening a stallion's ass
          as it breaks into full stride

there are crashes
      tires leaving darkened marks
        imprinting black top as fenders collide
        left mangled, intertwined

she tastes
      whipped cream sprayed from a cold can
      piling into the back of her throat
      lining her lips
         and its excess dripping from her chin

she feels
> the arctic chill of ice-capped waters
> budding avalanches repositioning her earth
> the sudden sweat of menopausal flashes
> boulders skipping down mountainsides
> a falling redwood crushing the forest green

there are no silk caterpillars
> creeping to the gentle tunes
>> of a woodwind orchestra
>> as dirt coats their bellies
>>> and its smoke fills their eyes
>> as they dream of the distant day
>>> when they shall be beautiful

instead
she experiences
> the boosters of rockets sending her pelvis
> into the stars to explore another galaxy
>> beyond her vast physical universe

there are no pastels
> only dazzling colors
> brilliantly vivid, unforgettably bold
>> with the cum-smeared haze
>>> of antiquated photography

for her
> the light grows brighter
> the sounds take center stage

and she is impeccably gorgeous
> in erotica as her big barrel is pounded

and its vibrations cover every inch of flesh
> in the heat of passion
>> she hears percussion

♥ ♥ ♥ ♥ ♥ ♥ ♥

𝕷𝐎𝐕𝐄... and do what you like
~ **St. Augustine** (patron saint)

Trouple: 3 Intimately

she was a Chinese finger trap
& this position was no mishap

an insatiable enjoyment was found
whenever she had both ends pounded

three hands were pawing prints
into her outstretched skin
as she laid unlatched
letting these less-than-gentle men in

this luscious receiver
was her tastiest/juiciest at this junction
a wise seducer
increasing her fluids & fruits for this function

upon her knees, she played the part of prey
being the merry recipient of two dicks in one day

ass opened wide & wet to #2
as #1 firmly held her head
all walls stayed slippery
as her four lips were spread

bent her back, extended her neck
showed amazing dexterity
glazed them in her sauces
while being penetrated simultaneously

she covered one with saliva
quickly oiling his prick till slick
as her butt cheeks
were repeatedly lifted by a merciless dick

#1 stood stern
carrying a girth-gifted piece of wood
#2 knelt at her rear
and dove a little deeper than he should

her arms balanced her dangling breasts
as she cheerfully gave her sensual best
to bring both fuckers total happiness

a sweet soul seeing submission & strain
as sexual pleasures
she believed in sacrificially sharing
her erotic treasures

volunteering for this, she had to be brave
had to have heart
being a middle-woman
she knew they'd tear her ass apart

perhaps she's a happy whore
getting what others wished for
to suck & fuck at the same damn time
who could ask for anything more

💋

Everyone has to make their own decisions. I still believe in that.

You just have to be able to accept the consequences without complaining.

~
Grace Jones
(Jamaican singer, model, actress)

ON

the sound of your voice
      tooting charisma in my ear
      shooting tingles down my spine
      sprouting cum creations in my coochie
                  turns me on

say those words sincerely
      brewing battles
           with my fear of falling for you

'cause you keep on
                  turning me on

oh yeah
      you best know
      that I know you're falling for me, too

hours of giggling
      has your mind reeling

my tongue-and-tail
      have got you guessing
how many miles is my place from yours
      where could you take me
           to leave an impression
show me how attentive you were
when I spoke of my favorite things

right now, you are calculating
when the move will be made
      to cut across my bridge
           and access my inner energy
      when are you going to ask me
           if you can stroke my ass
                  internally

what is it about you

I can't decide

whether it's your eyelashes
        or your narrow hips
the clean fingernails
        or the pinkish tone of your lips

        for some reason
                you relentlessly
                      turn me on

and I'm sharing
            personal shit
                prematurely
                      'cause I feel wrong
        treating you like the men
                who have moved on

so you alone hold records
and break molds

getting my home phone number
and stepping across my threshold
within days of that first hello

you got me
soliciting shyly but seriously
soliciting a preview of your privacy
wondering
        oh when are you going to share
        your hard rod with me
                    visually
        because I'd really like to see

but even sight unseen
I can already tell
it embodies the capacity to please

even if it ain't big
I know it's handsome
'cause you are
                    ...and you
                        turn me on
        keep giving me your best game

    'cause baby
        I'm waiting to moan your name

wow...
      damn...
          baby...
              yes,
    I keep thinking about you too

            and wow...
                you turn me on 👄

Six Senses {SMELL}

scented

the persuasive aroma of machismo

    flesh fresh
from the falling waters
  of a steamy shower

      cologne
on a crisp, pressed collar

       sweat
  pulled from pores
as he pumped her
  to the threshold
of another cumming

she missed the smell of herself
    on the upper lip
  of a lover's French kiss

she missed the smells of a man

INTOXICATED

as our lips part
as he walks away
i want more

>another soft kiss
>a cushioned embrace
>the comfort of his touch

minutes after tasting him
i crave him

>breathing deeply
>thinking of his lips
>our lips together

i sit in traffic
adjusting the mirrors and seat

>slowly i realize
>the mirrors never changed
>my posture has straightened

what an erection
his lips left in my spine

>he leaves me high

3 minutes of serious sex

and

I need
8 hours of sleep

and

a bowl of Wheaties

~
Richard Pryor
(comedian supreme)

My Body's Soul Mate

        certain weeks
     I wonder of different Willies
I walk throughout the minutes
      with my brain's spotlight
          being taken off target
            on an array of possible positions
                  if I made a transition
                  to the bed of another

        certain days
   I crave
the smaller man
     whose penis
          I can hold in the palm of my hand
              and
          I am preoccupied
     by its petite physique
          permitting a better blow job
              {and most definitely
                  some anal action}

        certain days
   I crave
the bigger man
     whose penis
          I must take the best way I can
              and
          I am blindsided
     by its bulk and drive
          the difficulty of total entry
              {and the inevitable need
                  to change positions
                  to regulate its pounding}

but for the last few
I can only remember you
          whose penis
            was proper in fitting
                my pocket oh-so-perfectly

you were the one particular
    who wasn't too tall
        {restricting my in-action activity}
        for the sucking of your nipples
            or the blowing of your neck

you were the one particular
    who wasn't too short
        {limiting my lovemaking}
        to the wavering of my breasts
            before your widened eyes

you were the one
    who was my body's soul mate
        and in the heat of the motion
            we fit fist-to-cuff
        since you were
            tall enough
                to reach my lips
            short enough
                to lick my tips
                    all while tapping
                    my ass non-stop

for the last few days
    I've been remembering you
        ...
    the man who fit my body perfectly

men aren't attracted to me by my mind
    they're attracted by what I don't mind
        ~
        Gypsy Rose Lee
        (ecdysiast <> striptease artist)

The Lesson

come near, Casanova
there is wisdom in my nudity

today's lesson
      is the gate of all humanity

it demands
      your undivided attention
      and requires all of your senses

permit me to lay down
      giving you the whole view
            of my spreadsheet

LOOK
      at its beauty
      intriguing layers
      an arrow of hair
            directs you to bliss
                  with clit at tip

TOUCH
      course exterior
      glistening interior
            feel free to
            unravel my thriller
                  with your finger

SMELL
      previous lovers
            deceived you
      but vinegar is only good
            for salads
      and potpourri
            belongs in a bowl
      allow me to
            relinquish the myths
            of dead cats and fish markets

   it's fresh
      with only a light scent
        to enchant you

TASTE

   see, Big Man
   sweet n' sour
      has nothing on me
   this is pure
      blazing sweet
        booty cream sauce
      {peppers buried inside}
      (available in mild
        for the weak-hearted)

FEEL

   penetrate me
      in search of
        my puddle's origin
   its glaze
      permits easy diving
   feel the heat—I warned you
      my jalapenos
        are making you sweat
   please...
      don't be gentle
   it is made for spirited plunges
        and baby birthing

HEAR

   the nectar
      greasing your head
      covering your piston
   listen
      to the popping
   and if you make it happy
        my kitty
   might purr for you
      she just may
        call your name 👄

fresh peaches

feel me
all over

ensure my readiness

cleanse and bloat my skin
with your softest touch

wet me
leave me slightly soggy

deliciously damp

now take me in your mouth
savor my flavor

overwhelm neglected taste buds
as the juice gathers in the dimple of your chin

dwell within my drippings of joy

like fresh peaches

the fact is I am not having sex
but I feel absolutely ripe for the,
what would you say? plucking?
~

Angelina Jolie
(actress, ambassador)

𝒞urv 𝒞ummentary

Better Blow
Tips for Oral Sex Enhancement

All recipients should be cleansed and cropped. The giver should be free of dental issues. Unaddressed oral infection exposes the receiver to bacteria and possibly blood. Oral sex includes body fluids. All parties should be currently tested. Otherwise, use precautions (a condom, dental dam, even saran wrap if you must).
Now on to the good stuff ...

> Cunnilingus (cunni): mouth on pussy: giving lip
> Fellatio (fella): mouth on dick: giving head
> Anilingus (anal): mouth on anus: giving rim

Here are a few pointers for enhancement:

(1) TALK – Inquire about the recipient's oral preferences. Favorite position is important but what about genital sensitivity (sucking intensity, fondling speed, tongue pressure). One must know if you like your clit/head/anus sucked, slurped, or stroked. What about penetration during elation? Ask about the ass.

(2) TOUCH – Feel around before you go down. The receiver has a neck, some nipples, and a navel between their lips and hips. Take a moment to nib, lick, and kiss along the way. Warm them up before blowing their mind.

(3) THOROUGHNESS – Cunni: A pussy should be explored from mons pubis to perineum, from top to taint. If you have never mistakenly licked a lady's asshole, you are

not giving supreme lip service. / Fella: A dick has 2 balls. Don't be afraid of the unit ... open wide and put it in your mouth. Play with its partners. Some men are very comfortable having their taint touched. / Anal: An anus doesn't require oral entry. You don't have to lick the hole. Just play around the rim. Note: Be mindful of your teeth. Cover them with your lips.

(4) TECHNIQUE – The tongue is the star of the show. Work on your skills. I recommend soft serve ice cream for practicing strokes (circles, up, down, side to side, or making figure 8s). / Cunni: Use a peach. Its juiciness and texture are good for coochie simulation. Cut a shallow wedge into it from top to bottom with the center slightly deeper. Learn to lick the entire opening. Use the extracted slice for clit practice. / Fella: Use a banana for tongue play. Test your tongue's flexibility. Roll it around the shaft, tickle the underside, suck on the top as if it is a dickhead. (Do not deep throat a banana. It could break off and choke you.) Use a peeled cucumber for throat practice. Relax your throat and slowly proceed. Test your gag reflex and strive to control the urge. Saliva is your friend. Wetter can make a blowjob better so the whole experience will glide. Practice breathing on the upstroke by pulling in air around the perimeter of the penis. / Anal: The anus has various textures as you move towards its center. Start with the lights on. Find your level of comfortable. Then circle away as your partner goes crazy.

(5) TIME – Make an appetizer feel like an entrée. Extend your timing by using your hands or a vibrator. Nails should be trimmed and cleaned. Make sure the finger is well lubed (saliva or water based). / Cunni: Chin and

nose can be helpful for clit pressing. Use thumb and index fingers to stroke the vulva. Insert the index and middle as the thumb rubs the clit. / Fella: Form a ring around the penis touching thumb to index. Grip his manhood firmly while stroking rhythmically up and down the shaft. Snuggle around the head before pulling through. / Anus: Check with your partner first. If the person is a newbie, start with the little finger. For a pro, use your thumb. But go slow.

(6) TOUCHDOWN – What is the goal of this interaction? Will there be a happy ending? / Cunni: Is the receiver one-&-done or multi-orgasmic? When she comes, she may not be done. Prepare for more. / Fella: Discuss in advance where to direct the semen so all parties are in accord. Will he shot for your breasts or give a pearl necklace. If he comes in your mouth and you don't want to swallow, keep a towel near to softly spit. / Anal: Orgasm vary by the participant. Some people come via their genitals during the act. Others require further motivation. Just ask.

**Practice will bring you closer to perfect
So practice, practice, practice.**

genital giant

urged to open her eyes
and see the plunger
he was placing inside

as the anguish of
previous moments materialized
in her mind-blowing references
of his wonderfully wide wand
she felt safe
behind her shutters

with him
there wasn't room
for fantasy
he eliminated
self-induced illusions
of the extra hands of a second man

in his pants
was a stick of supremacy
that banished
both desire and dream

there was only
him on top of her
making a ruckus
in his squeaking bed
and she was urged
to open her eyes

responding inappropriately
was not wise
for sexual disobedience
he truly despised

so his loss of courtesy
should have come as
no surprise

his voice
began to growl
his pumps
lunged aggressively
as he started to chastise her
for making him wait
for a chance to behold
his image in the dark basins
of her petrified eyes

he spoke as a parent
presenting reasons while
inflicting physical punishment

it was her fault

she was the reason
his dick did what it was doing

she was the complicated lover
who ignited the flame
and changed a sensual simmering
to a beastly brew

it was her

she was the reason
he was doing what he was doing
and his aggression
demanded her attention
as he urged her
to review, record, recall
the way he was tearing
down her walls

so according
to this man of cocky authority
she could open her eyes
witness the fucking he was laying on her
and receive minimal grace
or provoke the reckless penetration
of his prepared-to-punish penis 👄

WHY IS IT JUST AN ANNUAL
(dedicated to Dr. H)

females (and one feminine male)
handle his business
    before my pleasure
checking me in
        so he can check me out

escorting me to a numbered room
leaving a sheer robe
    with instructions to strip nude
                for him
my frilly exposed flesh
    tingles in the cooling breeze

subconsciously aware
    of the patients preceding
    and those who will follow
my forethoughts lie only in him assisting me

a knock (his knock)
and my heart's tempo is disrupted
    by the rhythm of his ratta tat tat

...it is him...I stop breathing...he pauses
then he follows his warning into the room

slowly he opens the door
    searching for my face
    looking for my eyes
    walking towards me and my nudity

he always starts by thanking me
    for seeing him once again
    for my patience, for entrusting him
    for the "ready to receive assistance" smile
            shining above my chin

he sits at my feet calmly
    asking me about my honey pot

genuinely concerned about my (her) health

"does she have a cold?
    any coughs, aches, or pains?
    has another professional examined her
        since our last rendezvous?
how many fortunate souls
    (with less expertise)
        have felt her vapors?
how did you protect this temple
    as they penetrated her pleasing quarters?"

    unlike my other lovers
he actually wants me to tell the truth

I tell him
    she hasn't been exercising regularly
        but I'm hoping that changes
            ...real soon

    congratulating my precaution
he rises from the chair bestowing his first touch

the start of our foreplay

    misted in the warmth of his breath
his stethoscope
    is lunged beneath my left breast
        directing me to breathe deeply
            exhale slowly
                (for him)

his other palm resting on my spine
the paper covered fingertips
    monitoring this rise and fall
        on my shoulder blade
he taunts me softly
    repeatedly saying "again," "again"
moving his hands
    to the various quarters of my happy back
    and different parts of my chest/breasts

"now please lay down
 (so I can get a better look at you)"

watching the skilled examiner
 rub his hands together
warming them (for me)
 my nipples enlarge
and he disrobes me
 moving the sheer divide aside

looks into my eyes
 before his next touch

asking if I touch them regularly
 (when he really wants to know
 if I masturbate)
as the tips protrude
 like clay on a potter's wheel
he glances at the provoked growth
 and grins

with his hands leaving my delighted breasts
 he says
 "place your feet in the stirrups
 slide to the edge
 (for me)"

our intercourse begins

he sits
perched upon black leather
 drawing the spotlight upon my she

focusing all his attention
 on my alcove of ecstasy
using his fingers
 to unlatch my gates (once more)

he slowly inserts his tool
its chill sends shivers
 through my vagina

the silver spoons
>funnel energy to my g-spot
>>while searching for my cervix

>>as he opens his guide
>I lay quiet and exposed before him
he peers into my gateway
>viewing my smiling cervix
(I've always wanted to see it
>does it pucker to kiss my lovers
>does it wink at the gynecologist)

like my licking lovers
>he too wants a sample for remembrance

with a long q-tip
>he rubs me internally
>>smearing my lubrication
>>across slivers of glass
>>to view me closer (later)

the creamy KY coated silver
>clanks shut
>as he withdraws it and rolls back

how special my body feels
as he stands between my open thighs
>delicately entering me with lubed fingers
>pressing his path into my sixth chakra
as my clit flushed with blood
>smooches his loving hand
>>>slowly

>>>(reluctantly)
he removes his splattered digits
as I exhale

>to satisfy the freak in me
he inserts his longest
>covered by cum and a little KY
>>into my tight ass

he's never explained why he does this
        (I ass-ume it's just to tease)
        contrary to its will
                my ass releases his retreating finger

removing his gloves
        he stands victorious
        knowing once more
                he has pleased me

        enjoying his courtesy
my manicured toes are lifted
        from the stirrups
                as I scoot back onto
                our table of enticement

bashfully
I gather the shredded robe
        like he hadn't seen my everything

acting innocent
        like this was our first time

        by my side
        deep into my eyes
he recites the regular salutation
as I grin warmly
        selfishly pleased and grateful
he thanks me
        vowing to do me again
                                next year

the door shuts
silent and stimulated
I remain immobile
        waiting for the aftershocks
                to subside
                trying to wind down
        in the heat of my annual paper sheet   👄

THE MAN IN ME — Kitty Passion

I love her pussy
the warmth of flowing cum
    my dick engulfed
        infusing its trunk
soaking my pubic mane
        and dabbing my testicles

I love the sounds of her pussy
the popping explosions it makes
        and the ones my fingers create
    my penis emerges from French kisses
smacking like a fish
sucking the surface of a pond

I simply love her pussy

loving her can't be wrong
she makes me feel desired
    how passionately
    her body accepts mine

she takes my manhood into her grasp
    and cradles it
she wants me and my fuck muscle
      (with her, inside of her)
she loves us and makes love to us

she sucks my dick sometimes
    (even if she don't really want to)
she loves us just that much
    and she never complains
she never demands, for that I feel grateful
    'cause I know she knows
        I love her pussy
    and I'll do whatever it takes
    to keep her (and her golden gates)
        in my life

Oral Orgasm

tonight
      prepare your lips
           with a thin layer of Vaseline

be sure to apply enough for two

I want to kiss you
      for a long, long, long time

I want to kiss you
      like I just fell in love with you

I want to feel our noses
      gently sweep across each other

I want to be so close
      that I see the grooves in your iris
I want to be so close
      that those light freckles on your cheeks
                magnify

I want to hold your jaw
      the back of your neck
           rub the top of your ears
graze your shoulders
      brace your spine
grip your biceps
      hold your hands
      as I kiss you
           again and again
           for the very first time

so please don't disgust your tongue

hide its taste buds
      behind peppermints and Listerine

I want to taste you
I want to explore your molars

outline the inside of your lips
    with the tip of my tongue

swab the points of your canines
    until you giggle
stroke the roof of your mouth
    as your tongue lies helpless

exchange saliva
    until I can't tell what is yours
      and what is mine

but I want to take my time
        ...uninterrupted
guaranteeing to my satisfaction
    that I tongue-fucked you
      like no other

and baby, don't close your eyes

I want you to see me
    fucking you orally
    screwing your lips
    humping your tongue
    fornicating with your orifice

I want you to witness my passion
      acknowledge my endurance
      commend my rawness

I want to see you breaking down
    with your eyes screaming for more
      as you tremble before me

    your tongue wild
    your lips impatient
    your body surrendering
      to my oral organ

    then just as you peak
I'll be your faithful freak
    licking you off until you cum

Sugar Smacks

it's my turn

a chance for me to cover your chest with kisses
as you've done mine
so regularly

it's my turn to plant smacks on hot flesh
bouncing with your heart's beat
just beneath the surface

my lips are ready to imprint your chest
for the pure pleasure
of pleasing you

let's began with some sugar smack appetizers
and as this evening's entrée
      I'll do you in any way
            you'd like me too

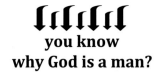

**you know
why God is a man?**

**because
if God were a woman
she would have made sperm
taste like**

chocolate

~

Carrie Snow
(comedian, writer)

HARD SHIP

allow me to assist you
handle your strain
prepared i am to bear
even your deepest of pain

let me volunteer this body
no other could handle you the same
pound upon my shores
compel me to orchestrate your name

because
i'm ready, i am ready
for your pressure, i must endure
this daintiness you see
is purely a part of my lure

place your hard ship in my tranquil waters
blend into the tide
anchor onto my rhythmic hips
move within my glide

as the waves grow higher
you'll elongate your stride
rock my boat, feel free to tip it over
surge deeper from the backside

with the release of your burden
i shall submiss
sweat from your brow
trickle to my back
crowning our bliss

hold me close—lean upon me
treasure me with your kiss
...and with a breathy sigh
i'll hear you whisper
"no relief was ever as good as this"

Filthy 5-Letter Favorites: ERECT

a sweet smile crowned by soft, dark brown locks
the doe-eyed, curly-headed connoisseur of cocks

she is a voyeur of viennas
a can-I-see-your-prick chick
who respects and salutes
the wicked power of a nice, erect dick

only special flagpoles
are introduced to her mountain top
and only a handful
have been used as her lollipop

a rarity who must see the chunky trouser snake
before she can totally appreciate
(the man)

so she is selective about the few who qualify
lustfully waiting for the right man to comply
boxers dropped by third date so she can verify
that his piece is able to visually satisfy
{though she refuses to date another Gemini}

**preferring a partner who is prick-proud
capable of knocking her ass
into the ninth cloud**

her lovers are never mean, disloyal, or shy
being touched, tasted, and licked bone-dry

adoring structure, curvature, tone
viewing each erection as a gift
discovering beauty in every bone
especially the ones she's fucked with

Piece-Taker

play the role of prey
           and lend me your ear

let my vernacular
        pluck the nerves
        connecting your mind
               to your nipples
               to your navel
               to your groin

my whispers
shall direct your attention to
        the brush of my breath
        the depth of my cleavage
        the heaving of my belly
        the bubbling of my private passage

and you'll be unable to turn away
      as I torment every cell in your body
      with every muscle connecting
           my piece-taker
           to your glorious formation 💋

**a woman's a woman
until the day she dies
but a man's only a man
as long as he can**

~

Jackie "Moms" Mabley
(the funniest woman in the world)

VICIOUS

at times
their sex would be vicious

it would be raw and dirty

nasty
filthy
gritty
tantalizing

it would be offensive, disturbing, animalistic
damn near illegal

he would rush her

pushed his firmness
       into the soft folds
              of her steaming flesh

she'd be pinned against the front door
       a stripped mattress
       the back wall of the shower

he would rush her
       render her helpless

her soft whine
       slowly escalating
            into a fearful shriek

but his pursuit
       would rapidly grow impatient

he'd take her
(though they both know
she wants him to do so)

rush her
mostly from the rear

he'd grind her
then swiftly seek
    her dampness

his stinger sought out her nectar
    with a vengeance
there would be
    a disrespect
        she'd subliminally enjoy

the entry of his dick
    into her dew
    would have a different tug
        and a delicate pull
as he pushed into her pot
    though the cream
        was not quite full

    pushed his way into paradise
    as she'd cry as he satisfies
at times
their sex would be vicious

it would be raw and dirty

nasty
filthy
gritty
tantalizing

it would be offensive, disturbing, animalistic
damn near illegal

at times, their sex would be vicious
    yet evermore delicious

Quoteworthy:
Lust vs. Love

Sex is the consolation you have when you can't have love.
~
Gabriel Garcia Marquez
(Columbian novelist, journalist)

The Bible and several other self-help or enlightenment books cite the Seven Deadly Sins. They are: pride, greed, lust, envy, wrath, sloth, and gluttony. That pretty much covers everything that we do, that is sinful ...or fun for that matter.
~
Dave Mustaine
(founding guitarist/vocalist of Megadeth)

**𝕷ust's passion will be served
it demands
it militates
it tyrannizes**
~
Marquis de Sade
(French Nobleman, novelist)

QUOTEWORTHY: Laughter

Sexiness wears thin after a while
and *beauty* fades,
but to be married to a man
who makes you laugh every day,
ah, now that's a real treat.
~

Joanne Woodward
(actress, producer, wife of Paul Newman)

Really,
sex and laughter
do go very well together,
and I wondered
—and I still do—
which is more important.
~

Hermione Gingold
(sharp-tongued English actress)

Pop ❋ Cum ❋ Snow

Twos
occasional threes
were presented
to her lips
      awaiting entry
    or
      coming right in

he would feed
      the exploded kernels
          to her
          to see
              the formation of her lips
                  up close

        (they were personal like that)

he would speak of the similarities

            ❋ popcorn ❋
              ❋ sperm ❋
           ❋ snowflakes ❋

all pale in color
all fluffy on the tongue
all unduplicated parts
forming a collective

he would press his body
      into hers
      to see the whiteness
          cling to her extended tongue
              up close

such a dignified pink arch
      slithering from its damp haven
          to await the arrival
              of white, light lust
                as he would stare in wonder

her tongue, again, for him
    becomes a tug
        known for offering smooth rides
                convenient hours
                superior service
      becomes a transport for pleasures
        to rub that dangling flesh
            at the back of her throat
            tickled last by his manliness

happy is he knowing his animation
    last entered this separation

    he was indulged
seeing the popcorn
    pass her lips
joining his delightfully deposited sperm
      and snowflakes licked from mid-air
            earlier that day

Semen Taste Tip
O O O   O O O   O O O

cinnamon, cardamom,

peppermint, and lemon

will improve the taste of semen

~

Daniel G. Amen, MD
(Dutch author)
Sex On The Brain:
12 Lessons to Enhance Your Sex Life

SUPREME BEAM (PART I)

      when I spotted him across the room
      I felt something sexual
      it took me a minute
      but quickly I knew why

I remembered
our unanticipated rendezvous
    happening on a warm fall night
        my jeans were tight
           g-string black
and I'd dropped my napkin
    just so he could see me
        bending from the back

after one thing
    kept leading us to another
        we agreed to escalate
    though our merger
        wasn't actually a date

maybe the moon
    was aligned with an impulse
        triggering our fires to rage
        igniting our cum to churn

maybe we were connected
    being in need
    of something new and unexpected

    so before the rooster could crow
I'd watched him
    lick me from his fingers

    and though we never
    were totally intimate
he deserves recollection

'cause he had the prettiest penis
        I've ever seen

SUPREME BEAM (PART II)

not being a man
      of grand stature
we stood
      toe-to-toe, eye-to-eye

so bright was his complexion
surely
he was the lightest kid in class
      probably the teacher's pet
being meek, mannerable, and
         oh-so attractive
            in a bookworm-ish way

he was humble as a lamb

spoke from his heart
      wooing me
        closer with soft words
          and eyes screaming
          of a sexual shortage

even though
I found him alluring
      feeling a passionate peace
           in his presence
I'd never figured
      him to be the carrier
         of a tool
           of such exceptional beauty

I'd never figured
      him to be so endowed
         so enduring

but he had a beautiful boner

and being an authority on this subject
being a woman bold enough
         to ask a man to see

I can say adamantly
    how extraordinary
        was the organ attached to he

  with such an unparalleled apparatus
      lesser men would be cocky
      and
      he, too, would have
        every right to be
yet he remained modest
as he whipped out
    his candy cane before me

upon its reveal
    I forgot how to construct a sentence
    I overlooked where we were
and it didn't matter
that I didn't know his last name
so
to this day
    I can't explain why
    I asked to kiss it

maybe
the width, length, tone
      swiftly got the best of me
for I didn't realize
      how beautiful a penis could be
even my most dynamic lover
      was suddenly secondary

truthfully I laid my lips on it twice
and I wasn't being proper or nice

something in me
    said I had to
    put my kiss upon paradise

 the first kiss
    in admiration
the second
    in gratitude

he had allowed me
    to see something
        justifying a chunk of memory
he showed me a rod
        finer than the best novelty
        a dunker deserving of my poetry
    in the docile
    (yet dominating) display
        of his extra-ordinary privacy

how delicious an instrument is woman
when artfully played upon

how capable is she
of producing
the most exquisite harmonies,
of executing
the most complicated variations of love,
and of giving
the most Divine of erotic pleasures

~

Kalyana Malla
(author of ancient Hindu erotic literature)
The Ananga Ranga

GLOSSARY OF GENITALIA

Vagina

fat rabbit ♀ honey pot ♀ Garden of Eden
baby maker ♀ home sweet home
Miss Laycock ♀ cherry stuffing
The Deep ♀ bikini bizkit ♀ velvet glove
cockpit ♀ sugar basin ♀ undertaker
Mary Jane ♀ gate of life ♀ sperm sucker
dick dungeon ♀ breakfast of champions
center of attraction ♀ sunny south
pussy ♀ love chamber ♀ va-jay-jay
organ grinder ♀ hoo-ha ♀ Peter's Grove
catcher's mitt ♀ coin purse ♀ tailgate
snake charmer ♀ Bushy Park ♀ neighbor of Anus
Davey Jones locker ♀ bone collector
furry furnace ♀ where the monkey sleeps
Courtney Cocksleeve ♀ sausage wallet ♀ oracle
poontang ♀ nature ♀ lady flower
python syphon ♀ bread winner ♀ juicebox
rocket socket ♀ nether regions ♀ cum craver
Temple of Venus ♀ cotter muffin ♀ liquid slip
you-know-what ♀ parenthesis
nappy dugout ♀ enchilada of love
Mount Pleasant ♀ sugared diamond
banana box ♀ lather maker ♀ grandest canyon
the black mouth that says no words
moneymaker ♀ cookie ♀ Hairy Potter
Fort Bushy ♀ scrambled eggs between the legs
happy hunting grounds ♀ fortune nookie
temporary lodgings ♀ Bermuda triangle
divine monosyllable ♀ furry pink mink
whatchamacallit ♀ Republic of Labia
Cupid's cupboard ♀ golden doughnut
meat counter ♀ vertical smile ♀ queef quarters
lover's lane ♀ tickled pink turtleneck
fuckhole ♀ meat curtains ♀ Cock Inn
eye that weeps most when best pleased

GLOSSARY OF GENITALIA

Penis

cherry-tree shaker ♂ whip ♂ tallywhacker
poontanger ♂ short arm/third leg
8th wonder of the world ♂ womb raider
Admiral James T. Cock ♂ Jack Robinson
all meat, no potatoes ♂ steamin' semen truck
hairy hotdog ♂ dooflicker ♂ free willie
beaver basher ♂ mouth plug
doughnut holder ♂ Pinocchio
Jack-in-the-box ♂ screwdriver
dick ♂ Kaptain Kielbasa ♂ twig & berries
one-eyed trouser snake in a turtleneck sweater
ham and two eggs ♂ yogurt shooter
woody ♂ anaconda ♂ wiener schnitzel
Longfellow ♂ tummy banana ♂ jackhammer
vagina miner ♂ love muscle ♂ ding-dong
poinswatter ♂ zipper ripper
slim reaper ♂ Johnnie ♂ deep V diver
kidney scraper ♂ quiver bone ♂ baloney baton
dickory dock ♂ lap rocket
sweet meat ♂ President Johnson
dude piston ♂ Jurassic Pork
cookie pounder ♂ dangling participle
groin ferret ♂ shaft of Cupid
split filler ♂ red-hot poker ♂ Pied Piper
pussy plunger ♂ Pennis the Menace
bone ranger ♂ pee-wee ♂ cervix crusader
hoe-handle ♂ dicktator ♂ Principal Skinner
snake in the grass ♂ fudge sickle ♂ muffin bruiser
meter long king kong dong ♂ nutty buddy
bushwhacker ♂ tube steak ♂ pink cigar
heat seeking moisture missile ♂ magic stick
kickstand ♂ beef whistle ♂ water pistol
chunky monkey ♂ Buster McThunderstick
Peter ♂ schlong dongadoodle ♂ ramburglar
family jewels ♂ arse-opener

Chapter 2

Deliciously Wicked

When Naughty Meets Nasty

Ain't Gon Make It

I ain't gon make it
I ain't gon make it
         to that sex deadline
we set while still in possession
              of our right minds

back when
     I was a bit afraid
     and you were a tad skeptical

we made that solemn vow
     before
     you started dominating
          my conversations
     after
     I started dominating
          your daydreams

but baby
prepare to bear
the burden of my persuasion
     for it has begun to strategize
     a few methods that'll make you
     want to have sex with me a little early
so today
     I can honestly say
         I ain't gon make it

eventually
     I'm gon urge you
         to put your hand on my hip
             strapping your spirit
             to the sway of my stride
     and you ... you about to be preoccupied
             wishing you knew
             how I felt on the inside

as my kisses
     become wetter, passionate, and long

your dick, oh your dick
    gon forever be hard as a bone
        'cause like I said before
          I already know
          I ain't gon make it

  by this time, next week
    you gon grow weak
  from my affectionate pouting and whining
you about to grow accustom
  to my compliments
      delivered in perfect timing
you gon grow fond of me
  and you and your magic stick
    gon want to be one with me
      (as I with you)
so when your balls turn the darkest shade
        of indigo blue
you and your dick gon figure out
      what I already knew
    that I ain't gon make it

darling let me go ahead
    and ask your forgiveness
    before I commence
      to committing the sins
        that's gon do you in
    before my tongue
      takes advantage of your neck
        and licks your earlobes
  'cause me and my kitty
      have set our own set of goals
        with an altered deadline
      and yours is so much further away
          than mine

so you best heed my warning
    for my hunt will be merciless
      ignoring your sanity's pleas
    'cause my hardened nipples
      keep driving wedges
        between my buckling knees

so
if you don't plan on getting fucked
you better stay the fuck away from me

otherwise
I'll greet you
butt naked at my front door
hold you to my bare bosom
until you beg me for more
and if that don't work
I'll spread my nudity
upon the foyer's floor
while asking how can such wetness
you ignore
'cause I already know
like I said before
I ain't gon make it

as soon as we get the results
of those sexual tests
I'm gon introduce you
to some of my sexual best

I'm gon give you
a parking lot blow job
that's gon make
your ass cheeks ache
that's gon make you
blow the horn by mistake
and even though
your ride gon be in Park
you still gon be
pumping the brake

so you can call it instinct
but sweetheart, I don't think
that you gon make it either

Quoteworthy:
Music

The sexual embrace can only be compared with music and with prayer.

Marcus Aurelis
(Roman emperor, Stoic philosopher)

Bed is the poor man's opera.

Italian proverb

SPIN CYCLE { 1/2 poem }

I can't knock
          what I haven't tried
and if I said I did it
          I would have lied

but you can believe I shall
          and when I do
I will tell the world
          starting with you 👄

I consider sex a misdemeanor

the more I miss de meaner I get

~

Mae West
(comedian, screenwriter)

SHARE YOUR SHIT

let's talk about
    your messed up childhood
    your fucked over adulthood
        and that time you learned
        something unforgettable in the hood

let's talk about
    tears
    corky ways
        and that body part
        you force yourself to love

let's talk about
    bad sex
    broken hearts
        and the hole you left
        in your last lover's windshield

(but do know... if you plan to fuck with me
    you can't be fucking with my property)

and while we're at it
let's discuss your dislikes
    your dissatisfactions
    and the ways you've discounted
        the love of other women
'cause I can tell you've got a mean streak
    supported by a couple of insecurities
so go ahead and share
    your selfish, lazy, trifling ass habit
            'cause I got one too
so unlike the women
    who've preceded me
        I want to know all about you

and just as proudly
as when you presented
    your assets and accolades
    (those shining stars)

tossed on the table to
        tempt me
                to sway in your favor
        tempt me
                to share my nakedness
        tempt me
                to start dreaming today
                of fucking you five years
                        from now

I want you to use
        that same sincerity, passion, and intensity
and
I want you to tell me
        what is fucked up about you

not just the fact
        that you refuse
                to put the cap on the toothpaste
                or the moustache trimmings
                      I can expect to see
                      sprinkled in my sink
I need to know more
there has to be more

        before I enter
        into this trial of my fidelity
I want to know
        exactly what I'm getting into

so share your personality trait
        that will
        on more than one occasion
        force me to say
        "fucked up" and your name
                in the same sentence

        and since I don't participate
        in one-sided relationships
I want you to
        know exactly who I am
        'cause I got my own shit

baby
you need to know
how snobbish I'm bound to respond
if offered a beverage in a plastic cup
           with a bite mark on the rim
even at your momma's house
I'm bound to get a little snazzy at the mouth

you need to know
that I'm a poet and forever I shall be
    so I'm gon write down
        your fuck-ups right next to my fantasies
           and by the time I'm finished
                I ain't gon give a fuck
                    how you feel about either one

but you really need to know
just how seriously I take sex
    to the point
    of putting the wrong motherfucker
        out of my house at the stroke of midnight
           in the middle of a blizzard
    and I still don't feel bad about it
    after what he did to me
    lying about his sexual abilities
    lying about what he could do to my body

now
before you donate
a chunk of your heart
    you need to know
    the shit I will do
        that will have you saying
           "what the fuck was I thinking
                when I hooked up
                    with your ass"
'cause baby
I got my own shit

darling
don't get it twisted
    I find you attractive

        and I believe
        you will be responsive to my kisses
                and the creeping of my fingers
                        up your inner thigh
but realizing
loving comes easy to the freaky
        let's start this thing off right
                push the alcohol aside
                grab a cup of cappuccino
for once
let's start at the bottom
        and shovel shit
        before we start plucking roses

let's put the cart
        before the horse

I want to know all about your Wiz
        before I start skipping all this ass
        down your yellow brick road

for once
I want to try something different
        as I get to know someone new
and fortunately for me
                that someone is you

now baby
come on and scoot over here
        I need you near
        sit back, relax, my dear
        but speak up and be clear
'cause you have some stuff
        I really need to hear

now tell me baby
        go ahead and tell me
                all about your shit 💋

hard lay on a hard day

tension
        is riding her neck
stress
        has attached
                to her lower back
life
        has started
                to twist a screw
                        into her spine

she is pissed off
        to the highest level of pissivity
                (as robin harris
                      would say)

and she needs
        a helping hand
        to push the grayest clouds
                      away

this is one
    of those times
        when she needs a rush
        of something new
            to occupy her mind

so she'd like it...rough

hold to her hips
        like she stole something
                from your grandmother

collide into the fattiness
        padding the back
                of her thighs
        like she owes you money
                (and your rent is past due)

it has to be...rough
       to shake loose
       the heavy darkness
       weighing on her chest

you have to forget
       your manners
and disregard etiquette

hard...and please don't quit

don't stop...no time soon
       'cause for you
             her body
             is making room
             in its sauciest of spaces

       and if you
             do her
             the way I say
you could see
       her thighs
             grow red
       her nipples
             grow hard
       her spine
             grow limp

don't stop

think not
       of quitting
             and be not kind

she wants you
       to be a little forceful
             with your fitting

this is one
       of those times
             when she'd like it...rough

3rd Glass Of Wine

all limits
>had backbones built of flexibility
>in their sexual escapades

abnormally nasty were they
>freaky & free to explore more

maintaining
a practice of colorful games
>>one was called 3rd glass
>and it always ended with him
>>fucking her in the ass

she would on occasion
>have that extra drink

>>intoxicated, purposely inebriated
>>easily persuaded, willfully seduced

he would assume
>the kitchen cleaning
>>that evening
as she'd proceed upstairs
accompanied by that 2nd glass
>for a bath in a warm stream of bubbles
>to rest upon her blushing flesh
>>in preparation
>>for their rambunctious reunion

he'd appear in the door frame
>toting a chilled glass
>>of grapes' blessing

>she would be lotioned
>>(moist on the surface and internally)
>primed for his touch
>>sprawled on their bed
>>reclined—ready to be seduced

with smooth steps
        he'd come to her side
                placing her 3rd glass of wine
                        on the nightstand
he'd bend to kiss her lips
        as his middle finger slid into
                her liquid slip

he'd survey its slow withdrawal
        standing erect before her
        placing her appetizing juices
                upon his tongue
                as he proceeds to the bath

        by the time
        he emerged
                from the bellow of steam
she would have
        candles lit
        ass greased
        her hot points perfumed
                and the wine consumed

a mix of music spinning
        sensually supportive tones

later
after foreplay is finished
        as he's deep V diving
                his single-minded hardness
        into her cream filled pocket
they shall shift suddenly
        during the rhythmic rowing

        ultimately
his wood will fall
        from her vagina
                bumping fiercely
                      into her asshole

        but instead of backing away
        to reset his aim

he will press forth
    and a little wider
        shall she open
           allowing the head to slip in
                as the anal fun begins

and the next day
    rising in the renewal
        of their nocturnal nastiness
they shall blame their exploration
    lacking customary hesitation
        on that 3rd glass of wine 💋

MISBEHAVE SOUNDWAVE

which tone turns you on?

sweet names like "baby"
or
nasty slurs like "fucker"

☺   😐   ☹

moans & groans
or
soft scratches & screeching screams

☺   😐   ☹

the breathless whisper of your name
and the smack of juicy kisses
or
*the clash of sweaty flesh
and the harmony of sticky cum*

☺   😐   ☹

which tone turns you on?

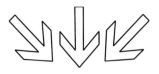

GODDAMMIT

get that pussy off the table

{seated next to a feline, Cordelia hops off the table}

I was talking about the cat

~

Irene
(C. C. H. Pounder)

(Guyanese-American
film and television actor, philanthropist)
*Tales from the Crypt:
Demon Knight*, 1995

STEAM

I was rushed
          at unexpected times
          in the oddest of places

he'd come to me
          quickly
          prying into my panties
          begging entry...yet again

and since his routine
          demanded my participation
        I perfected my part willingly
        I would give into his appeal
          let him happily play
               in my lukewarm steam

he never twisted my arm
      only promised to do
      my booty a little harm
                   ...so I'd let him

      years later
      I learned
why he'd step to me
and push my undies aside swiftly
      to dive
         into room temperature pudding

slowly he'd enter me
      when I wasn't boiling hot
               or dripping wet
      to see chips of cream
               he couldn't forget

those small chunks
          sprinkled along his dick
captivated him
          as he stroked his stick
          in my coolness

this warming process
        changed my chill to a simmer
                and
he would witness the rising
        of my coochie's core temperature

steady were his strokes
        churning curds to cream
                and finishing in a glaze
it was my metamorphosis
                keeping him amazed

to see and feel
        this evolution
                of sweet agony
                      gave face to his wildest dream
the manual process
        of his red hot poker
                popping my ice
                      until it turned to steam

♥♥♥♥♥♥♥

sex is not the answer

sex is the question

" Yes "

is the answer

~

Swami X
(psychedelic hippie comedian)

Anything Like Me

if you are anything like me
    you look at
        your family, friends, coworkers
    even total strangers
        and try to figure out
        their preference for pleasure

    oh, it would seem
        too simple to simply
        think of their nudity

'cause
you'd rather think of
    their moments
        of masturbation
    their secret stash
        of sexual stimulations
you'd rather
    picture them fucking
        if you're anything like me

{you're scoping
people's stares for
    how they'd view
        erotica vs. pornography

you're scoping
their smiles for
    how they'd appear
        after an orgasmic earthquake

you're scoping
folk's laughter
    for a glimpse of
    how they'd respond
        in ecstasy
        to their fancy being tickled}

surely, there isn't anyone else like me

    who's cool with your best friend
        sharing the details
            of a romantic evening

    but
you try to rush pass
    the roses, the cuisine
        the plot of the play and the attire
    you want to know more about that fire
    and you ask in a roundabout inquire
like
how did the evening end
did he tap your rear end
    and if this was the first time
    would you fuck with him again

'cause if you are anything like me
you waiting for the right person
    to drop their keys
        just so you can watch them
            bending over

you at the family reunion
    trying hard to control your lust
but you can't stop
    imagining a full frontal thrust
as your cousin's sexy-ass spouse
            walks to and fro
you remember busting a nut
    to their memory about a week ago

if you're anything like me
you're welcoming conversations
    about the beauty of cum
        on your fingertips
    your favorite places for a quickie
    and what structurally
        makes a dick
            so damn pretty

surely there isn't anyone else
    'cause
if you're anything like me
 you love to see
    folks eating soft-serve ice cream
    and fries with too much ketchup
and you're waiting for
    the lick of a finger
        or the cleaning of lips
and swear you can tell
    how they look
    while fucking and bucking their hips

but
surely, there isn't anyone
    who wastes their time
        wondering, pondering
        about other folks' fucking

surely, there couldn't be…
    unless
    you are anything like me

❤❤❤❤❤❤❤

**does thinking about sex
all the time mean
there's something wrong with me?
do most women weigh up
the fuckability of every man
they meet?**

~

Abby Lee
(author, blogger)
*Diary of a Sex Fiend:
Girl with a One Track Mind*

freak's bizarre

with a band of bizarre appeals
a gang of inquisitive curiosities
        reside behind his innocent eyes
for his freakiness resembles a clown's car
packed with an endless parade of characters
        who seem to surface
        from the shadows
           of his enticing carriage
and you just happen
to have cum upon him
        in a period not permitting
        frequent practice
           of sexual playfulness
his hunger
began to growl
        so he sought release
        in a parade of exuberance
           that a domineering woman
                such as you
                could feast upon 👄

Six Senses {TASTE}

a sample

As she drove, her beau's persistent begging became unbearable. Ambidextrous. She held the steering wheel with her left, unzipped with her right to coat her middle finger in honey.
Happily quieted, he sucked her digit clean.

YA DAMN RIGHT
(in honor of the Egyptians who originally invented the condom)

I'm human
>> forever sizing up folks around me
>> forever questioning
>>>> the next man's point of view

that's 'cause
I'm curious
>>> wondering what you think of me
>> as I guess on a whole lot of shit about you

> so
if you've written me off
> as a damsel in sexual distress
>> awaiting an adorable dark knight
if you figure me to be
> the pillow top phoenix
>> perched and ready to take flight
if you believe
> I'm equipped to get my freak on
> cum day or cum night
>> I'm here to tell you
>>> that ya damn right

somebody has concluded
> I'm prepared
>> at a moment's notice
>>> to fuck a chosen few
somebody's figured
> I'm preoccupied
> by thoughts of making love
>> whether sitting in traffic
>>> or on a church pew
and if you're guessing
> that my closest girlfriends
>> are only told
>> a portion of the freaky shit I do

so being a little promiscuous
    I'm always toting a condom
                or maybe two
    well, good for you
        because
            ya damn right

who knows what might
    happen tonight

a muscle man could text me
        a teddy bear kisser could call
I could be on the other side of town
        with my back against the wall

with the future
    so unpredictable
I might run up
    on a kissable, lickable
    lovable, dickable
        that I really like

better yet
    I might run upon an old flame
telling me
    his sexing remains the same
he just might remind me
    how paint used to peel
        when I cried out his name

or I could cum upon the one
    who knew how to use
        his thing right
he may remind me
    that when I saw his dick
        it was love at first sight
who knows
    he might guarantee
    that the penis is smooth and tight
        just like I like
who knows
    what might happen tonight

so if you think
I'm the kind of woman
who has a condom
                in her pocket
                        right now
                        ya damn right

when midnight come calling
        there's no telling where I'll be
        there's no telling who I'll see

I may be cuddled up
        with a gentleman groomed
                for an evening of good luck
       there may be a stallion
            in my stables who's worthy
                      of a memorable fuck

what if I hook up with a lover
            cute, confident, and free
his words could
        strike the right cord in me
and I believe in being prepared
            for life's pleasant possibilities

because
I'm a lover of the lovely
and for that right fucker
            I'm an overachiever
      a 24-karat giver
            but a platinum receiver
but rest assured
        that I'm also a cautious diva
avoiding bumps and babies
        as I seek out my pleasers

so if you are thinking
                I can be enticed
        by a hefty package
                and a smile really nice

if you believe
        for special occasions
                I keep a sock
                        ready for the slipping
        and for the rare rendezvous
                there's always a rubber
                        ready for the ripping

if you've concluded
I'm the sucker
        who told her man
                "a blow job
                can be given
                in so many places
                        ...let me show you how"
so I'd most likely
        be the kind of floozy
        who'd have a condom
                      right here and right now
pat yourself on the back
                stand up and take a bow

because it's my pleasure
        to inform you that
                ya damn right 💋

I love bald heads and dreadlocks.
Saints and sinners.
I love them light, bright and dark as night.
I love them sweet and strong.
I love them all!

~

Sheryl Lee Ralph
(actress, singer, activist)

Do you know...
THE BASES

1st base
KISSING

2nd base
TOUCHING

3rd base
TASTING
FINGERING

Home
SCREWING

Meek the Freak

if not so private, quiet, meek
they would label her a freak

humble in word, demeanor, attire
leaving so much more to be desired

a woman of biblical fortitude
restricted, serene, lackluster attitude

apart from thrice a week
when all have laid to rest

an unknown caller
would enter her minimalist nest

and the whole neighborhood
against their will witnessed her vocal best

frigid women
considered her boisterousness
a pest

their men
lying awake
envying the unidentified midnight wrangler
she has chosen to bless

**THERE ARE THINGS THAT HAPPEN IN THE DARK
BETWEEN TWO PEOPLE
THAT MAKE EVERYTHING
THAT HAPPENS IN THE LIGHT
SEEM RIGHT**

~

Erica Jong (author, educator, poet)

INSTEAD

8 days from this dreary Friday
she's decided
      to let you enjoy
      a section of her
           that you've never known

she's decided
      to let you adventure
      in a section of her
      that none could enter
           unless she was drunk or stoned

she's decided
      to bite the mighty bullet
      and let you cum
           through her back door
      let you step through an exit
           you've never entered before

      a lavish palace
           she's saved for last
8 days from this dreary Friday
she's decided to let you
           fuck her in the ass

8 days from this dreary Friday
she is going
      to inform you casually
      that she's washed herself clean
           both inside and out
      she's going to share with you
           the position
           she's been dreaming about

for the greeting of
      your stunning masculinity
she's going
      to wear something seductive
           and make you hastily

            rush through your meal
            rush her through your front door
            rush her body to bend submissively
    with no resistance
    and let you take all of her
                    from the back
                    and through the bottom

she's going to let you
        creep inside her caboose
                and experience the tightness
        of her freed anxiety
                at a time
                when she'll be fresh
                            out of sobriety
she's going to have you
        making love
                to her ba-dunka-dunk
        till the motion
                starts rattling the junk
                        in her trunk

8 days from this dreary Friday
        she's going
        to have you making love
                        to her posterior
        she's going
        to make you fall deeper
                    than you envisioned
                    the day before

and you shall see
        her back stretch
                as if she's on the verge
                        of giving birth
        and you shall hear
                a melody of moans
                sounding unrecorded
                        and unrehearsed
she's going
        to give you the keys
        to her backyard sanctuary

which means
    by the break of dawn
you would have had her
      in every possible way...

she's going
    to have you
    breaking new ground
      (in a place
      usually sparkling
        in a Hershey brown)
    and you are going
      to be speechless
      as you discover a new means
          of connectivity

8 days from this dreary Friday
she's going to clap a new thunder
        make a different rain
    with an experience
      reserved for the insane

8 days from now
as she undresses on the way to your bed
she's going to say
    "don't worry about my coochie
    I want you to fuck me in the ass
        instead"

♥♥♥♥♥♥♥
thanks
I enjoyed every inch of it
~
Mae West
(sex symbol)

Filthy 5-Letter Favorites: TAINT

(noun): the flesh separating genitals from anus

velvety lube came easy on wings of lust
flowing like melted ice cream down a cone
fresh nut butter would start to churn
reminiscing about his succulent honey bone

butt it wasn't only the penetration
satisfying her sexual expectation

it was his good-ass head
that kept her juicy ass laid up in his bed

**there's a difference
between tickling twat
and eating pussy**

and he knew how to eat some pussy

taking his sweet time to dine
between her outstretched thighs

nose peaking over her bush
as he stared into her eyes

butt sometimes, he'd lick her
madly/gladly front and back in one sweet accord
butt sometimes, he'd cross her taint
pushing her calves toward the headboard

because he knew to keep a nice lawn
he'd sometimes have to cut some grass
and to satisfy her orally
he'd occasionally have to lick a little ass

teetering

she'd forgotten
the thrill of having her core breached
                her innards displaced

he dared her body
        to delay its submission
        to defy or deny his will
     rearranged her organs
     shifted their familiar foundations

he'd tossed them up

open thighs
     exposed her private passage
         to activities happening
             so infrequently

some of the shifts
     had to be remembered
         in the midst
            of his invasion

he bullied
     her gullible physique

his dips sprung roots
     digging deeper
     enforcing his demands
         on her limited internal garden

marvels were performed
     on her body
         provoking her vagina
             to thunder
        as her mouths experienced
             wet (lower)
             and dry (upper)
             simultaneously

as she accepted the euphoria
of physical torture
by a monstrous penis
as she swung on the brink
of ecstasy's insanity

he misplaced her vocal cords
in awe of the unspeakable
as he teetered a brick's throw
beyond her internal perimeter

the difference

between

pornography

&

erotica

is

lighting

~

Gloria Leonard
(pornographic actress)

WISHFUL THINKING

the core of your fascination
but he is not as affectionate with thee
strictly my friend, no desire to be one with me

in the dark and day, you've envisioned him
in your most intimate places
touching his cheeks, softness of his flesh
as he inhabits your deserted spaces

blessed thoughts of his babies
he sports the shining armor of every dream
the husband you've awaited
with another woman turns your heart green

so you view me as a threat
to your lopsided dreaming
wish he would distance himself
you start plotting and scheming

wanting to insult me, you throw shade
"oh I forgot your name"
knowing he's memorized my phone number
has driven you insane

as you touch him with two fingers
not realizing I've held him with all ten
no need to tell, where I'm sitting
is the spot you wish you were in

this isn't the Olympics
no race to run, prizes to win, or victories
free to select his companions but
you can't see him beyond your fabricated stories

the woman I am is naturally sexual
making men happy is part of my flirt
you must return to reality, accept your position
    'cause even imaginary love can hurt

Our Founding Fuckers

Vanessa Del Rio

She is a role model
for every woman
who wants to express
and enjoy her sexuality.

~
Foxy Brown
(rapper, model)
Vanessa Del Rio: Fifty Years of Slightly Slutty Behavior

Alfred Kinsey

If Kinsey is right,
I have only done what comes naturally,
what the average American does secretly,
drenching himself
in guilt fixations and phobias
because of his sense of sinning.
I have never felt myself a sinner
or committed what I would call a sin.

~
Mae West
(singer, sex goddess)

INTERVIEW WITH A MASTER

a master

an expert in the field
of intense physical gratification
    offering a curriculum endorsed
        by elite pupils
    worn-out, sweaty, and smiling
    offering no tangible agenda
        specifying courses
            deemed necessary
                for certification

instead he spoke
    of his endorsed endowment
and he sensed my hesitancy
    to register
    as I commenced to withdrawing
            my application

I told him
    perhaps I could settle
    for a Bachelor
        with erecting potential
        easier lesson plans
        a less strenuous learning curve

he replied
    it would be
        less lucrative
        less educational
        less rewarding
            with its minimal demands
he hypothesized
    it would eventually
        become unfulfilling

being a creditable Master
    I could tell this same lecture
        was given before

he asked
        for effort and submission
                flooded my ears
                with soft spoken possibilities
                        of enrichment

he said my credentials and assets
        made me one of only a handful
        qualifying me
        exclusively
                for his program

        though his exercises
                are difficult
                and he is meticulous
he said there will be
the availability of tutorials

and extra credit
        remains optional
        for the improvement
                of my GPA
                (Grind Precision Assessment)

                leaning closer
                looking deep
within my eyes of fearful curiosity
he asked me
        to give him
        an opportunity
        to boost my skill set
                and yield to the chafing current
                        of his abounding wisdom

        he could teach me
how to prepare
        for an encounter etched
                by an extraordinary lover
how to submit to
        the philosophy
                of permanent change

if I enroll as the supporting actor
of his cock's cabaret
I must strive to be teacher's pet
in hopes of an ounce
of my professor's empathy

I normally
don't do interviews
with women
unless
I fornicate with them

so you shouldn't talk
anymore, unless
you want to,
you know

...
~

Mike Tyson
(world heavyweight
boxing champion)

SADISTIC STAR

    vulgar

the mass-dong man
    gorging upon
the unadulterated outcries
    of his overly penetrated bedmate

his piercing eyes
    seating atop flared nostrils

her appeals for mercy
    falling upon his deaf/sarcastic ears

his enlarged one-eyed demon
    stretching her cunt's chimney
        beyond its natural brink

    past life
this well-endowed brother
    was probably
        the king's henchman
        the controller of the guillotine
    then his smaller dick
        hardening with
        the blade's incessant journey

    modern day
he penalizes his costars
    feeding his demonic appetite
        on flesh seeking freedom
        from his sexual fiery

    centuries apart
that same insatiable spirit
    has flourished once more
        to please a cheering, lust-ravenous crowd
        of dirty-minded, sadistic hell wishers 💋

THE MAN IN ME | Holding Me

as the streetlight
peeked through the blinds
    I was hitting that ass from behind

when she *ssshed* me
for a second we paused quietly
    then she started controlling
                  physically
    and the only explanation given
        was a statement to calm me

she said
    "baby, let me hold you
    permit me to squeeze this rod
            gently
            sweetheart
    as I please myself
    with a dick top shelf
        until my cum gates part"

she said
    "baby be still
    allow me to do as I will
    and I promise you'll feel
        real, real, real good"

in the sweet orange hue
peeking through
    I saw my queen
        from a different side
    I stood stiff and strong
    as she took my bone
        for a joyride

muscles started to tighten
    the moment heightened
    euphorically dizzy and enlightened

remounting, she flipped the script
    her dominatrix spirit took control
enabling me to see the shadows
    surrounding her darkened booty hole

slowly she made circles
        in the midst of midnight
her undertaker bringing my longfellow
        sheer delight

displaying acrobatic complexity
slowly the grind gave way to gravity
cream descended down my shaft rhythmically
she began to blow my mind in her fucking simplicity

using skills to rebirth a position we usually do
I experienced her familiar jelly roll anew

as her walls crawled down my shaft
she released mms followed by a laugh
        followed by an inhaled grip
        followed by a syrupy internal slip

the fresh wetness coated my pole
    new lube set her bounce free
it made her bang even sweeter
    as the nooky turned velvety

the blinds made strips
    on the back of her outstretched hand
as her massage of my shin changed
    from loving screw to fucking romance

since that day
    longfellow has been hypnotized
        by my baby's sweet hold
now he surrenders
    and stands tall in two ways
        letting her undertaker take control
        when she whispers
            Baby, Let Me Hold You 💋

𝒞urv 𝒞ummentary

EVERY BOOTIE

 does <u>not</u> belong

in pornography

DISCLAIMER: The following statements are not meant to be cruel.
Physically, we do not construct ourselves.
But we do decide to what extent we will share our nudity.
If you are a member of the pornographic society
and any of these factors apply/offend you, I apologize.
This is simply one person's (humorous) opinion.

My expectations are really low when I first pop in a pornographic DVD. It's a blind purchase; no reviews or recommendations given. There is no thought wasted on the quality of its script or décor. So as my new flick loads, I don't swim in the "anxiously awaiting this experience" euphoria caused by an award winning film.

The movie was purchased in hopes of getting my rocks off. I bought it because something on the cover (its title, a descriptive phrase, or maybe a few photographs) aroused my libido. Then my monkey begged me to bring it home.

Nonetheless, I do believe that the actors should be porno-worthy. Anyone showing their ass for recording purposes should be stripper-material. Thus, having good body structure, minimal scars, and tantalizing genitals. A porn star should be the type of person that a large group of people would enjoy seeing naked and sexually active. Every filmed ass must remember that job performances are being recorded for massive review.

Realizing perfection doesn't exist on Earth; there is no notion of flawlessness. However, I would appreciate a higher degree of standards during the selection process. Because there are times when I find the actors in a dick flick to be distracting.

Let's start with normal-yet-irregular genitals like super-sized clits and elongated nut sacks. Have you ever looked at a zooming camera shot in horror? Unconsciously wishing the lady's clit wasn't really that big, hoping there's a fingertip next to it? Then watching her partner sucking it and having flashes of a miniature prick?

Personally, I hate when balls block the view of connectivity while resembling mid-July fan blades in public housing windows. On several occasions, I've seen dudes with low-hanging balls revving up their strokes and bam!...scrotums become helicopter propellers. This lack of visibility destroys my voyeuristic bliss and ticks me off to the highest pissitivity.

there are certain visuals
I don't care to see
when attempting
to set my monkey free

I also find tattoos to be inappropriate when they are too large and/or located in the wrong areas. A R.I.P. tribute on the back of a riding stallion is a distraction to the action. How long has the person been dead? And how were they related? How did they die? Or a unisexual name like Demetrius scrolled on the chest of a dick-dominator. Is Demetrius male or female, lover or child? It forces me to forget the fucking and unconsciously ask questions. I want to know about the personal life of the star of the show instead of focusing on what I really bought the disk for.

But more than misplaced ink, I hate fake moans. I can't stand to see a woman with an oversized opening trying to time a small penis's penetrations. Or a soft penis being handheld to maintain insertion. Either way, the female's sound effects and faces of false pain remind me of old kung fu flicks. Her mouth moving at the wrong time like the fighting masters.

Forgery of fucking should be forbidden on film. It is so obvious, senseless, and a waste of good recording.

Then, there are the men with bumpy booties, the razor-ridged coochies, and hairy ass cracks. You get the picture. Elaboration isn't necessary.

But my biggest porno pet peeve is lazy fuckers. If a person lacks flexibility and stamina, they shouldn't be in the industry. Who wants to view a fat man sweating profusely while trying to dip his dick shaded by a protruding pot belly into a coochie hidden by thunder-ravaged, dent-damaged thighs? I can get that kind of fucking at home. Let me see folks who sweat more at the gym than on the set. Let them show me some new moves that I'll try soon and my lover will never forget.

> *filmed fuckers shouldn't show up*
> *if they aren't going to show out*

Of course, there are exceptions to this personal philosophy. My beliefs become flexible when medium-dented donkey asses, animalistic dicks, and amazing sexual skills are involved. But I still believe that fucking on film should be done by people who are in the higher percentile of fuck fantasy. Individuals who are well equipped and maintained.

If you watch porn, you've seen examples. Some folks should have thought twice before entering the pornographic field. Every call girl and gigolo can't successfully cross the line between screwing in privacy and nudity memorialized eternally. But all joking aside, I know no one chooses their body. However they do choose their career. And honestly, every bootie does not belong in pornography.

7 Things I Hate To See In Pornography

"extra" ordinary genitals

misplaced tattoos

bumpy booties

razor-ridged coochies

hairy ass cracks

fake moaners

lazy fuckers

VETERAN VANITY

in the smoky nightclub shade
    his onyx aura
    defied the weaker darkness

    there was steam
    emanating from his flesh
keeping
a smoky cigarette's murkiness at bay
    generating a perimeter of clarity
        to outline his sinister stiffness

lights of brighter colors
    strayed beyond the dance floor
        across his stature
white beams revealed his wrinkles

but with a blatant stare
I was washed
    by the lust in his eyes
        full of vulgarity

he saw me
    as a wish for younger days
    when his hips reinforced the words
    swirling from dark lips
    when his penis was plumper
        with the power
            of physical endurance
        as women begged for breaks
            and fell asleep thirsty

    if the sun's consistency
    had not betrayed him
he would have slithered up
    behind me

         placing the heat of his steel
            at the crack of my ass
he would have slithered up
         behind me
         blowing his peppermint breath
                  on the tense sections
               of my shoulders
                     melting away my woes
                     loosening the protection
                           of my panties

from across the room
I could fully feel his fantasy
as he stared at me hungrily
         and wished
            for one more younger day 👄

♥♥♥♥♥♥♥
it is not enough
to conquer

one must know
how to seduce

~

Voltaire
(writer, deist, philosopher)

How I Like It

their conversation skimmed sex
        but stayed on safer subjects
finally he asked of her desires
        asked her to open up
        and tell him what she likes

she took a deep breath and a swig of wine
blinked a few times...and said

"if you prefer a woman to lead in the bedroom
        telling you what to do, a dominatrix
        who grabs the headboard
        and rides you till you cum
                i am not the woman you seek

i prefer being the fuckee and not the fucker

i enjoy
        lying on my back
        on my side
        on my breasts
                while being fucked

i enjoy
        calling your name
        cursing your name
        screaming your name
                while being fucked

i enjoy
        oral sex
        regular sex
        (occasional) anal sex
                as long as it ends
                        with me being fucked

when submitting your sexual application
        please don't lie
'cause the short in yard
             and weak at heart
                       need not apply

i like a man who is up for the long haul
can't be reserved 'cause i have to feel it all

the pumping, the pounding, the thrust
ride me hard like i like and i won't fuss

if you like the motions of a big ass butt
i promise to enjoy
            the beat of your slapping nuts

i'm open to toys and tie-ups, i'll admit
and since i have long hair, feel free to pull it

do what you feel
        leave your handprints on my ass
i'll let you do it again
              if you don't cum too fast
              'cause i enjoy being fucked"

♥ ♥ ♥ ♥ ♥ ♥ ♥

there is nothing wrong with going to bed
with someone of your own sex
people should be very free with sex

<u>they should draw the line</u>

at goats

~

Elton John
(flamboyant pop superstar)

They All Want To See

every man
    (heterosexual that is)
    longs to see
        a woman climax

seeing peace
    sweep her face
    as his key unlatches
        her heavenly gateway

feeling her pelvis
    pressed forth
        for her clit to kiss him

    thighs shaking

hearing breaths skipped
    seeing her face shift
        across carnival mirrors

holding
    her stiffening body
    as a velvety volcano erupts
        at the tip of his penis
    its trembles
    spreading to toes, tips, tits
    her parched lips
    spewing his name
        followed with a curse
            or a prayer

every man
    (heterosexual that is)
    longs to see
        a woman climax 💋

Six Senses {SEE}

whom shall he love

Her belongings were now in the trunk
as her car pulled away from the curb.
She was driving and crying
as he stood arrogantly on the sidelines
and watched her weep.

Arms folded across his chest
beneath flared nostrils.
He felt powerful because he had choices.
And he'd chosen the other woman.

The falling sunset framed her departure.
Its dying dusk carried her into a new dawn.
Suddenly single, full of uncertainty
simmering in a pot of new insecurities.

A cool breeze crossing his shoulders
provoked an unexpected sadness.
The wind submerged its chill
into his selfish soul.

Regret began to smother
his blazing fire of conceit.
He had a sinking feeling,
questioning the basis of his decision.

Suddenly, he regretted words of agony
said in an air of superiority,
and words of love never spoken.
His eyes began to swell.
His head started swimming.
He kept seeing the pain and color change
as he turned her brown eyes blue.

fantasy #8   { 1/2 poem }

stripped of her will

blindfold
leather straps

hands unable to reach
for her trusty lover
knees pulled to the headboard
pillow elevated hips
fully exposed

HELPLESS

happily you dine on her delicacy
of blooming orgasms

*Sex is always about emotions.
Good sex is about free emotions;
bad sex is about blocked emotions.*

~

Deepak Chopra
(Indian-American physician, holistic health author)

Can't Help Himself

he
licks his lips
holds the bottom one
with his teeth
quietly starts panting
hands stretch

enthusiastic

saliva builds
heart pounds
eyes squint
blood rushes

restless

spine lengthens
trousers stiffen

as I walk toward him
he can't help himself

I've done things to that man
things that made his toes curl

I've made him shiver in my heat
forget his worries, live in the now

filled him with my total satisfaction

when he sees me
he envisions those things
and the joy they bring

overreacting?
no

he just can't help himself

She Winks, He Smiles

as words of his expertise
were being written
    he was thrusting the cum
        out of her
she was letting him
    look into the eye
        of her asshole

an opening
    that has winked
    at a group
        of fortunate few grunting guys
and
he's trying
    to chisel a new passageway
    through her paradise

now she turned her butt and back
    to his banging
    reinserted his axis
        again and again and again

    she spun around
    and placing her journal
    between his knees
so he could see all he pleased

she was letting him
see that ass bounce
    from the perceptive
        of a stallion's saddle

she was galloping
to his moaning amazement
    as he witnessed
        yet another side of her
            while she pleased
                her lover man

and every once in a while
    she'd stop writing
    she'd stop rocking
    she'd stop grinding

every once in a while
    she'd stop doing him
        just long enough
        to look over her shoulder
        and see her man's smile 👄

Conversation,

like certain portions of the anatomy, always runs more smoothly when lubricated

~

**Marquis de Sade
(Geoffrey Rush)**
(award-winning Australian actor)
Quills, 2000

SAP DRUNK LOVE

a day of harmony

while rays leap sweat-moisturized shoulders
she smiles and kisses you

summoning recollection of your alliance

and she is free
both spirit and body

intoxicated by you

   your soul
       whispers to her
           even when your lips are closed
sipped until saturation

trusting you with her altered self
you set her Nikki free

I know I'm seen as a romantic type.
But I like to consider that
life is a romance.
Whether I'm with someone or not,
I am romantic to myself.
~

Leon
(one of the Sexiest Actors of all times, singer, songwriter)

JURASSIC

you lay open wide
        before his demonic eyes
        as a grin of glee
                arouse upon
                        his face
        as he pushed
               his sexual solidification
                      into a hole
                      made of dampened walls
                            that he's inscribed
                            but shall never see
        (yet he's found pleasure
                      in its mystery)

the soft sheets
        covered the mattress
                beneath your spine
                and his knees
        as you accepted his thrashing

your moans encouraging
                his pounce

your milkshakes formed puddles
        as your ass was shredded
                in a position of submission

your breasts
        shook with each reproach
        reflecting a rhythm
        conducted by his wand
                in a musical duet
                      with your pelvis
        and each pounce
                caused them to jiggle
                      just like the puddles
                            in Jurassic Park

as you play the role
    of luscious earth
and he began to rampage
    shaking all
    that is within his reach
        causing your dark-centered puddles
            to duplicate the downbeat
            of his whipping wand
                within your wonderful
        causing your breasts to tremble
            like the puddles
                in Jurassic Park

❤ ❤ ❤ ❤ ❤ ❤ ❤

**it is impossible
to obtain a conviction for sodomy
from an English jury**

**half of them don't believe
that it can physically be done**

and the other half are doing it

~

Winston Churchill
(British officer, Prime Minister,
First honorary citizen of the US)

BACKSTAGE PASS

and his grip
became stronger
with every comment

                      "ssh ...you better hush, girl
                      ...folks are going to hear you
                      on the other side of the world
                ...baby it's okay...I got this...loosen up
                    you can trust me with your butt
              ...let me put this Frankfurter in your bun
              ...let me enjoy a little backstage fun
                        ...you can't tense up
                ...can't let this anal opportunity pass
          ...calm down, baby...so I can get a little more
                       of my shaft in your ass"

her diaphragm crawled closer
to her swinging breasts
as pats matured into plunges
and he became the storyteller
at the anal assembly
adding spicy commentary
to their bum-fuck

how rare she'd let him plug her derriere

every blue moon
she cared less and less
about the awkward stares
from adjoining units
sharing her condo's common walls
ignoring the looks of those she knew
weren't getting any action at all
so on these special occasions
she would wail
...and he would taunt
...and their neighbors would listen
        (as their wishful genitals thickened)

QUOTEWORTHY:
Pleasure's Price

Sex is like art.
Most of it is pretty bad,
and the good stuff
is out of your price range.

~

Scott Roeben
(comedian)

I believe that
sex is one of the most beautiful,
natural, wholesome things
that money can buy.

~

Steve Martin
(comedian, actor, playwright)

PREMIUM PUSSY
is like access to an exclusive club.
It cums with a cover charge.
In some way, you can expect to pay.

~

Curv Brown
(performer, erotic artist)

Filthy 5-Letter Favorites: PUSSY

you need to stop talking
so much about little dicks

you need to talk about big pussies

your grandmama don't like
when I say pussy

but

ain't nothing nasty
about pussy
as long as it's clean

~

Sweet Papa
(the sweetest man I've ever known,
my grandfather, age 77)

𝒞urv 𝒞ummentary

The Benefits of a Small Dick

*multiple factors determine the sweetness of a honey bone
the depth of a short leg is not dictated by length alone*

I can't lie, size is relative. Unfortunately, men have no input on the penis they received at birth. If they could choose, they'd all be real big and extra-long. But there is good in all forms of wood.

Marvels of a Mini-Magic Stick

❤ inconspicuous
a small package is easily hidden
if it hardens in an inappropriate social setting

❤ easy-to-jack
an undersized semen shooter
can be jerked-off, requiring only short strokes

❤ ACME (anti-choking mechanism)
a petite penis can fit easily into the mouth
of a gag-reflex sensitive person

❤ intensity without injury
rough play is permitted with no worry
of damage to the love pocket

❤ terrific for slipping through the backdoor
a perfect fit for buttloving

Even though size is relative, you must be realistic. As a full-figured woman, I must speak up for the voluptuous girls in the world. **Please remember:** *A good-sized woman with thighs of thunder and an apple bottom can automatically cut an inch off a dick on impact.* So keep this in mind when you holler at a thick chick next time.

But the pleasurability of a penis is also dependent on the pouch it is penetrating. You must consider whether your genitals are compatible. So, if you take a dip in a sizable hole and lose your pole, just move on. It's okay.

However those short-changed in length and/or stoutness must think outside their cocks. Remember: men have control over sections of their sensual existence affecting their overall penile experience. There are factors beyond performance capable of adding weight and appeal to a short leg.

The Best You Can Be
factors every man can control

**being a good eater
can make up for your peter**
study the sensitivity of your partner's genitalia.
where are their nerve endings concentrated?
depending on your preference:
practice on soft serve ice cream or a banana
until your strokes are perfected.

have a diversified sexual portfolio
learn a variety of positions
that allow your penis
the best penetration.
but learn to read your partner.
which positions best hit their hot spot?

don't gain a lot of weight
a big belly reduces the reach of your rod.
tightened abs allow for full accessibility.
also, if you like your companions
a little thick, stay fit so you can get to it.

Chapter 3

Screw-Arounds & Let-Downs

Cheating Lovers / Sorry Fuckers

i love you too much to...

if we make love, there will be memories
filled by smells and tastes
♥
hands longing to revisit my skin
lips yearning for my wetness
your erection desiring only my resolution
♥
there's an aftermath with every orgasm
there are consequences to such indulgence
♥
'cause if i make love to you, i will fuck you up
♥
only being honest
don't mistake my words as mean
i'll make you delay on washing your ass
as you lick mine clean
♥
get ready to lose track of time and direction
remembering you were running to the store
as you park your ride outside my front door
♥
so go ahead, start contemplating your commitments
'cause you couldn't fuck me all day
and sleep peacefully at home
you'd worry about my pussy; is she really alone?
♥
to get next to me, takes more than
a few clever comments or a stroke of good luck
there are qualifications, thorough evaluations
I must make sure you're ready for a platinum fuck
♥
oh, to the average joe, I'm a sweetheart
but when we enter that bedroom
I become a sexual beast
♥
so you can just drop your drawers
and show me that dick
because I can't even like you

unless I fall in love with your piece
♥
be prepared for me to leave you
with your fingers and toes numb
the stroke of my hand will have you dumbfounded
wondering where did all this cum just come from
♥
my thick love will even dominate your tongue
so get ready to call your girl my name
my sex will leave you stupid
you could never think the same
♥
therefore, i'll spare you some therapy
i won't allow you to make love to me
♥
'cause i love you too much to…fuck you up

👄

THE P WORD

rarely has this happened before
only under extraordinary circumstances
has a man ever made her feel like a whore

but a brother just achieved this feat a second ago
he said "ah baby, can I have some pussy"

unfortunate was he
to not understand the error of his plea
immediately
but he quickly caught on when she said "excuse me"
and her neck did a 180

a curse-out did not follow
there was no screaming and she surely didn't holler

she whispered him to shame
told him he better not ever call her vagina
out of her name

{which happens to be Luscious}

being a sexual missionary, she felt it was her duty
to educate the brother
         on how to properly address booty

"sweetheart, to avoid my reaction
you must not jump to such conclusion
don't crown yourself king
        in the midst of your own illusion
a true lady must grant permission
        for you to call her paradise
                'a pussy' in her presence

she may beckon you to say the p word
after making her
        shiver, stutter, break into a sweat
after pumping her to the brink of tears
        on a night she'll never forget

as you crack her spine
and blow her mind
        as she makes those oh-ah sounds
        while being licked or dicked down
        pressing her pelvis into your penis or face
amid a heated hallucination
        she'll tell you in a breathless haste
she'll say something like
'no one has ever done my pussy the way you do'
        she'll give an inviting clue
then and only then
can you consider yourself certified
        to use the p word
        the way she's been longing for you to

so without this prior authorization
    dare not use it, such assumption would be absurd
don't mistakenly think you are stimulating a true lady
    when you're just vulgarly abusing
                the p word"

Puppy In The Window

speak truth to her, pet

your credentials
    are easily forthcoming
        for this impromptu interview
    boasting your tale of mastery
        on the tails of many women

your hope for her employ
    standing on the wings
        of your spoken words
    as she scans your forehead
        for the words skipped
        and tucked away
            in the tightness of your chest
            as you freely share the rest

there must be reason
    for your loneliness
        even for a single season

there is something
    you are hiding
        'cause selfish
            are your wishes
            to entrap her heart
    before your hidden downside
            turns her away
            on some later day

speak truth to her, pet

why are you available
    what is the making of your core
how did a woman willingly
        walk out your door
how is a coolness allowed
    to settle on your charismatic sheets
        restless from single body heat

you have an idea
        what's the cause of
        your past lovers' change of heart
you know the details
            you seem pretty smart

speak truth to her, pet

are you jealous-hearted
            or envious, mean
       crude, touch too much
            or love too little

is your energy...low
        or your stamina...too high
            for the average female

is your Johnny short
        or your Henry too wide
        or is it curved deep
            to one side

something
        has caused you to be alone
tell her the truth, pet
        before she takes you home

♥♥♥♥♥♥

Sex shouldn't be comfy

2½ feet of irresistible, tubular sex

. look to the heel, young man .

the sex is in the heel

~

Lola
(Chiwetel Ejiofor)
(film and stage actor)
Kinky Boots, 2005

Filthy 5-Letter Favorites: TRAIN

on boys night out, a pact of partners
found exceptional pleasure
in the purchase of mutual pussy

none was desperate, unattractive, or antisocial

most had a woman of some type
(girlfriend, fuck-buddy, wife)

though a lover may reside in the same residence
they'd all buy a trick, chipping in on the expense

they enjoyed the savoring of
a crème-filled, unattached twat
each knew the other's package
so they'd wait their turn with the sexpot

drugs weren't the motivator in the girl's world

to her, only dollars and condoms made sense
but one of the boys would always resent
(his position)

possessing more penis
than most females found of good use
he was never the engine
always the unanimously-chosen caboose

only he and the man at the head of the train
could think somewhat sexually the same

knowing dick is distributed on a bell curve
so the first and the last
are the ones left disturbed

the first with the petite penis
gets the coochie fresh
though he can't truly screw it best

and the last may carry a 10-lb. Johnson
hanging closer to his feet
**butt by his turn, he has learned
the trick is never a treat**

2ndman (PART I)

(if my lover only knew the things we do)

who am I cheating as I make love
                          to my 2ndman

is it really wrong to give up ass
                      2nd hand

he makes it so easy
      never saying no, never trying to fuss
plus
      he never pries in our business
            (could care less about us)

          is he wrong for touching me
          am I another man's property

he has learned my body...
              inside and out
discovered places
        you know nothing about

blame me not for the need
        to have another man
              show and prove
he nicknamed me Stella
          after locating my groove
I find him insatiable
          and love to see him move

           beneath, behind, and above
so who am I really cheating
          every time I make love
          (with my 2ndman)

2ndman (PART II)
(my lover's secret assistant)

I'm the woman of a traveling man

try and try as i might
        to get this single sexual partner stuff right
I still hate to wait for his affection
        and sleep alone too much for my delight

though a ho
        I shall never be
occasionally
        his stays get the best of me
so on moonless evenings
        I grow weary of me pleasing me

and the longing
        for the cologne of a man
                drives me insane
this urge
    persuades my fingers
        to dial the number of 2ndman
                      once again

though he is not exactly
                what I'm looking for
questioning his sincerity every time
        I walk through his door

I can't stand
the thought of anyone besides 2ndman
        putting their unknowing hand
                (in my velvet glove)

2ndman is familiar
        with my sexual desires
                and my body's terrain
thoroughly sweetens
        my cherry pudding
                with his sugarcane

besides
he's equipped with a low-hanger
      escalating him above average
      controlled by an oral appetite
           that borders on savage

    so yet again
I find my shivering body below 2ndman's girth

sweaty and bare
      he stares at me after remixing my earth
with a confident air

2ndman sees pass my dishonor
      keeping his superior seduction within reach
for him, I can mentally justify
           an occasional breach
             (from my real man)
and I ain't going nowhere else
    because he, my 2ndman
        satisfies all of my sexual demands 💋

QUOTEWORTHY:
Trickery

All lovers swear more performance than they are able.

~

William Shakespeare
(England's national poet, playwright)

Men can't instantly change their size or stamina so why do they lie about it ?

~

Curv Brown
(creator of mentally-stimulating and crotch-motivating poetry)

Quickie Questionnaire

far from a porn addict am I
personally,
it isn't my libido's motivating preference
because...I think too much
and unless
I can quiet the avalanche of inquiries
to focus on the fucking,
I find porn to be an agitation
to my erotic meditation
at times
even the most skilled dick-layer
with the sweetest mouthpiece
can't hold my concentration
I find my mind drifting into unintended areas
of these videoed confrontations
as my curious observations

become assessments
which leaves me feeling silly
for secretly watching strangers screw
thus my thoughts destroy my peace
as I watch people get a piece
and my concern drifts
beyond their booty connection, easing pass
the point of poker piercing honeypot
because...occasionally, I think too much
and enjoy it too little
while witnessing the stimulations
of repeated penetrations,
I find myself distracted by my...

Pornographic Preoccupations

◊ why is pornography so male-oriented
from the initiating blow job
to the money shot finale **?**

◊ when did they start turning tricks for money **?**

◊ who encouraged him to enter this industry **?**

◊ were they both sexually violated as children **?**

◊ how old is that girl with the flawless skin **?**

◊ why don't women get head anymore **?**

◊ how much older is that man
and exactly how long is his penis **?**

◊ in the midst of the madness,
is she regretting the contract
she signed for this session,
suddenly questioning the recuperation
of her ass elasticity **?**

◊ exactly how many women has he fucked **?**
< I've seen him with at least
a hundred different women >

◊ is this encounter ruining or satisfying her soul **?**

◊ are her outcries real and are his grunts genuine **?**

◊ was she a stripper or a prostitute
before agreeing to be forever captured on film **?**

◊ why don't heterosexual men
wear condoms
like the homosexuals do **?**

◊ will she need reconstructive coochie surgery
after fucking that super-sized anaconda ?

◊ is that painful pleasure or bitterness in her eyes ?

◊ was she stimulated before the filming
or pumped full of bottled lubricant ?

◊ how do their parents feel
about their career decisions
and what kind of work
do their kids think they do ?

◊ how are they treated at their reunions ?

◊ filmed fucking is extremely profitable.
so are they exchanging ass
mostly for the cash ?

◊ how much does this industry pay for
butt-and-torso jack-offs
versus facial money shots ?

◊ what's the standard wage for
vaginal insertions
versus vaginal/anal combinations ?

◊ what is the pay differential for
one-on-one sexing
versus
ménage trios
versus
gang banging ?

HOMEWORK ASSIGNMENT

What are you thinking now ???

take a moment to reflect
on your own mindset
whenever you are exposed
to visual pornography

...

Now, go ask somebody ...
when you see folks fucking,
what do you wonder about?

RESERVED

as mute
    she is supposed to
        lay her treasure chest
            in his "knowing" hands
        observance of its total exposure
    mesmerized his mind
    allowing him to feel the various textures
        select her gems for his using
    quench his thirst
            with her savory chocolates
as mute

they said
    she can be great
        at cooking and homemaking
        intellectual at work
        motivated at the gym
    totally inferior is she to his wisdom
                sexually

they said
    he could teach her of her desires
    she should allow him to fumble
        (as she remains humble)
    believing to be amongst her first
    and accept that she wasn't amongst his
    so he would feel good about himself
        being the mind reader of many
        (occasionally satisfied) women

they said
    she can't control or move or moan
                too much
    any thought to know herself
        may classify as whorish
        will categorize as "known"
    he'd assume she'd been had by plenty
        and a real lady limits her exposure

as mute
>   she finds no pleasure
>   for this is her shrine
>   and the voice she possesses
>   can't stay still and fake happiness
as mute

>   if he intends to visit her shrine
>   she shall tell him
>   where to lay his head
>   when to enter her bed
>   how much of her he'll be fed
>   for she's been with herself
>   long before he knew her
>   and she must remain true
>   so she can't pretend
as mute

let there be
pleasure & ecstasy
on Earth
and
let it begin with me

~

Annie Sprinkle
(performance artist, sex educator)

Goodbye, Goldie

                                        irony stabbed
                                        its awakening
                                        into your ego
deflating the trance
you held over me
a year ago
                        you...you were the man!

the passionate phantom
    who showed me
        a new type of gluttony
    who modified me
        made sex a physical poetry
    who heated me up
        until my skin sizzled
    from stanzas
        of your lovesick melody
you took me
    on safari tours
introducing me
    to freedom, rapture,
        and acceptable reasons
        to overlook biblical laws

you took me
    on stages
    where porno is made
    (we just didn't have the cameras)
    where a lady imitates a whore
        and a man forgets his manners

you set fire to my bush
    curling my toes
    sweating out my hair
    and molding my body
        in a variety of sexual positions
        many allowing you to observe
            flames shooting
            from my own derriere

so it was ironic
for irony to catch you
    with your dick limp
    with your eyes hollow
    with your heart heavy
        and your soul questioning
        the validity of your loving
    realizing I'll soon leave your bone alone

you
the man whose penis
    was named after a pimp
stood before my bathroom sink
    and pondered if you were the one
        who got played

    with bulging presence
the evidence of another man
    stared back at you

towels you claimed
        (but never paid for)
    were posted next to mine
        and having learned me
    you knew this only happened
            when I was sexing

plus
the silver toothbrush case
    was a dead giveaway

far too flashy for my flavor
        and so unfamiliar

boldly
it stood out on a counter
    full of products
        you were used to viewing

maybe I've underestimated
    the power of your prying eyes
perhaps

             you peeped
                the condom wrappers
                        sprinkled in incense ash
                        lounging carefree
                                in my trash
during our session
        did you notice a difference
                in the tightness of my ass

regardless the clue
I know you knew

somebody
        recently
                touched me
                the way you were so use to
        and saw me
                combust
                in a way witnessed by very few

so it's ironic
        that you
                the one who claims another
        stood still
                amazed that another brother
                entered this stable
                and laid pipe
                        in your part-time lover
                enjoying the treasures
                        you diligently
                                uncovered

you stood astounded

swept away
in true fairy tale fashion
        'cause in the midst of our finale
poor Goldie started to see
        there was a new man
                laying in the bed
                        next to me   💋

Quoteworthy:
Size

Sex is like snow
you never know
how many inches
you're going to get
or how long it will last

~
Unknown

**Condoms should be
marketed in 3 sizes,
jumbo,
colossal,
and super colossal,
so that men
do not have to go in
and ask for the small.**

~
Francis Picabia
(French painter, poet)

your boo
left her boo-hooing

why isn't your man
laying in her bed
bringing her joy
as she gives him head

waking her with a morning treat
a soft smile with merry kiss to greet

an urge to feel and be filled
covers her constantly
with dread
runs up her love trail
to take cover
in her forehead

why is the pillow
next to her empty
no impression of where
his head should be
his body isn't curled up
next to her
no warmth, no stroke
no ecstasy

for a few stolen moments
they embraced
in a fleeting time
but he went back to you
now she can't get him
off her mind

why isn't your man
laying in her bed
bringing her joy
as she gives him head

Filthy 5-Letter Favorites:
Freak vs. Whore

"Whores always envy women who have the faculty
of arousing desire and illusion as well as hunger."
~ Anais Nin – Book: Delta of Venus

freak — available to one lover unrestrictedly

whore — obviously available to everybody

o

whore — does not worry
about her sexual performance
(focuses on the fuckability of her latest fucker)

freak — perfects her skills
for the thrill of a blessed few

o

freak — usually a lady
except for the private preference of her lover

whore — rarely considered a lady
(devoured by too many short-term lovers)

o

whore — has sex to get material things out of it
(can easily trade getting-bucked for some bucks)

freak — has sex for the joy of ding-a-ling
(money given to her is a bonus,
an offering of gratitude)

o

freak — can look nerdy, seductive, or natural
but never ordinary

whore — can only look nasty
(no matter how clean or stylish
there is always something about her
letting you know she's easy)

Snake In My Grass

a petty thief of pussy
    my aunt should have warned me

a man of low morals
    and strong-arm tactics

willing to fuck over
    his own mother
        for a fresh chance
        with a slice of rabbit pie

incapable of caring
    about my long-term happiness
he is the cobra of my cookie
    existing in the right here
    ready to bite right now

lusting
    like tomorrow he can't live
    if his dick doesn't explode
    once every 24 hours
        with or without
        a trick being present
            (and exhausted)

he is a selfish man

his snake slithers
        in my cave's creek
and the strokes start
    my ass to rattling
snatching air from my lungs
    leaving cramps
        in the soles of my feet

but in the end
    when he's posted up at my rear
the morality and common sense
        I care not to hear

a thorough lover
      is hard to find
and his match
      I've yet discovered
so against my will
      I crave him
because he moves me
         like none other

he's the snake in my grass

I was a slut.
There will always be
a part of me
that is dirty and sloppy.
But I like that, just like all
the other parts of myself.
...
Can you say
the same for yourself,
fucker?

~

Tiffany
(Jennifer Lawrence)
(Best Actress for this role)
Silver Linings Playbook, 2012

HE CALLED TODAY

how can you explain to
your man

                        that this other dude
                              has done you
                        like none other can
                        and he called today

how can you tell
Mr. Reliable that

                      Mr. Unforgettable
             asked to enter your door
                and you're not sure
                 if he was referring
                 to the wooden one

there's an oath of honesty
a pact between you
and your man of reliability
to be truthful

                        yet this other lad
              laid Eve's apple in his lap
                   and dared you
                      to retrieve it

                this orgasmic mystery
      resurfacing from your sexual history
         requires very little instruction
            and no introduction
               to your g-spots
             previously chartered
          on his erotic expeditions

         he makes you happy repeatedly

                        there's no way
          to describe the spells used
          that keep you hypnotized
       keeping this blast from the past
        forever tempting to your ass

                              to speak
                 of his sinister screwings
                    would take all night
               this man could do you right
            he made you bow before his might
                       and he called today
                 asking to see you tonight

                           how can you resist
                              one who chases
                       tension from your body
                          with a single kiss

                                    how can
             you discontinue longing emotions
           for a man who feeds you sex potions
           who rubs you down with slippery lotions
                       who made you a believer
                            in the existence
                      of mind blowing orgasms
                     and unexplained emotions

how can you explain
to your man today
              that you should have warned him about
                              yesterday's king
                       who holds a season pass
                           to your queendom
                   who has introduced an array
                  of new things to your ass

how can you tell your sweetheart
that today
you received a phone call
from your wild card
                 and he still holds a large portion
                                   of your heart
                                 and this could
                     tear your new thing apart
                                      because
                              he called today

                              👄

                              153

*C*urv *C*ummentary

PORN HAS PURPOSE

i watch porn
with a real purpose in mind

i stare at the screen
in glaring anticipation
of prepaid emotions becoming real
when the couple forgets
about the exhibition money
and start enjoying what they feel

so i sit patiently
flipping through scenes
until i come upon
a noteworthy encounter
once the cum
starts cumming down

i look for that split second
when the male's rhythm
catches the tail wind
in her tail end

such genuine display is a rarity
but it does happen

watching other people do
what they do
causes me to reminisce about
what I've done
my scenes and partners
also changed
with many moments
qualifying as undocumented porn

i watch porn
with a real purpose in mind

looking for that split second
when the female's faint moans
grow to whimpers
blooming from her quivering heart
when his instinctive dominance
aligns with the feminine energy
being released by his counterpart
as they connect on the same wave
and sail off to an orgasmic beat
as his groan-full groove
pounces upon her cherry sweet

to see someone screwing
starts a personalized slideshow
of memorable lovers
who aligned with me sexually
achieving similar results
with my body

plus pornography can provide
tips for future fucking

there's help, info, and enjoyment
in sexual cinematography
so most of the time
i'm scoping pornography
with a purpose in mind

are you normal?

as you pass
a magazine stand blazing with booty
or as sticky hot pieces of lust-filled porn play,
do you too find it difficult to turn away?

when the preacher
damns the world for its wicked way,
do you too have little
or nothing to say

thinking of the flick
you enjoyed yesterday?

but is it really wrong,
to see two people getting it on?

what if the sexcapade is
without exchange of disease,
without the production
of undesired seed,
without a misgiving of lust
to fill some emotional need?

to watch, is it still wrong
for grown folks to share a bone?

isn't pornography
simply fornication on film?
a recording for voyeurs
instead of a private session
between her and him?

if they aren't violating laws,
hurting and humiliating the innocent,
who are we to judge how they live.
if you don't like pornography,
that's your prerogative

as adults,
we have the freedom of choice
and even a closet freak
has a voice

because

pornography
is a multi-billion $ industry
providing a sexual supply
for an ever-growing,
increasingly-horny demand

I love everything
about giving oral sex.
The smell, the taste, the way
her lips and clit grow
as I work them...
The way she moans
when I make
my tongue hard
and stick it in her cunt
or lick her asshole.

~

Felice Newman
(Publisher of Cleis Press)
The Whole Lesbian Sex Book:
A Passionate Guide For All of Us

I'll Lease Your Man

In the presence of possibilities
I choose to play the role
Enjoying both passion and profit
While privacy remains my goal

I'm just leasing your husband
For a moment, for the night
Wholeheartedly we make love
Never do we fuss and fight

I know his place in my life
So I never wear lipstick or perfume
No need to send him home
With grounds for you to assume

No marks for you to find
Not one scratch, smack, or hickey
As I exclusively and joyously
Remain his darling Nikki

Did you once do the things I do
Say the seductive words I've spoke
Were you his initial fantasy
Over time became a ball-and-chain joke

I surrender with abandonment
Anything he ask, I'll do
Even in the shower, I appease him
And I swallow too

But I never kiss him on his lips
For fear of kissing you
Rarely discuss your relationship
How you look, I haven't a clue

For a maintenance fee and one day notice
I continue to be accommodating

Preacher would call him an adulterer
I'm no more than fornicating

Most people frown upon my actions
Calling it whoring or prostitution
See it from my point of view
It is simply pleasure retribution

We meet at my place
Lay in my bed
Mess up my sheets
I welcome him
And the dollars
Carried by his manicured feet

For hours
We use my home
Prophylactics, water, wine
He merely finances my labor
Like any employer
Paying for my time

Our desire is unmistakable
Our contract is invisible
I will give him elation
In exchange for his deliverables

I am that special woman
He can walk in and out of my life
Happily lightened in load
Returning to you, his clueless wife

♥♥♥♥♥♥

when he's late for dinner,
I know he's either having an affair
or is lying dead in the street
I always hope it's the street

~

Jessica Tandy
(English theatre and film actor)

Passing Plastic

in the midst of my nudity
the man disgusted me

      he hopped out of bed
      dug through his dresser drawer
      whipped out an unwrapped wand

    is he recycling the wrong type of plastic?
      am I, I must be dreaming?

walking towards me with rod in hand
                      my temples caught on fire
my eyes bulged, my waterfall dried
            his actions sopped up my desire

"how dare you pull out a piece of plastic
            previously used on another pussy"

Freaks

(like this guy I meet once named Alabaster)
have crossed my path
whispered secrets
and left me speechless

i may jot down my fantasies

but there are people without pens
who are far more freaky in action
than i could ever be in writing

~

Curv Brown
(wordsmith fascinated by fucking)

Six Senses {HEAR}

one word

being the first time
allowing your touch
please know
this much

if this two-letter word
leaves my lips
while you are poised
between my hips
think not
what's next on the menu
all action should cease
all motion must discontinue

tonight
the one thing standing
between stop and go
is the word
"no"

The Business Transaction

kaleidoscope of temptations
    lured them with its neon lights
their hearts galloped
    to the music's pounding delights

trixie strolled and shimmied
    through a drinking hole's darkened den
searching for the hungry
    willing to exchange her assets for dividends

"bartender, give me a double"
    she needs something strong
        to loosen her backbone

scope the joint for victims
    yearning for her affection
look for a bank roll
    next to an erection

one capable of paying
    for the promise of penetration
for trixie's guarantee of sexual elation

"loosen up, daddy, come...
            come dance with me"
she'll smell his desire
    and hold his penis internally (for a fee)
"don't be afraid, I don't bite
        you can hold me, baby"
john tried to believe trixie liked him
    tried to envision her long-gone virginity

"please understand i am only doing this
    because granny needs heart surgery"

besides, it was Friday
    he had two fat rolls
        in his front pocket
        so she'd do the smaller first

later, in a seedy motel
trixie was accommodating, the perfect whore
beating...beating...beating down
                  ecstasy's door

as trixie's breasts rode waves
            before john's widened eyes
"nasty little boy,
      you like the clash of my ass
                against your thighs"

it was too late when
      john saw the gleam of the blade
trixie slit his throat, ear-to-ear
      he was dirty, he'd misbehaved

as his final tear fell
      and his soul began to go
her scarlet lips informed him
      "granny died 5 years ago"

he paid the ultimate price
      for his lust-driven hyper-sexuality
john was chosen by a hooker
      with a serial killer mentality

♥♥♥♥♥♥♥

As a Succubus,
Lilin usually had her choice of any man.
They were easy creatures.
A naked woman and immediately
a man hardened in greeting.
She would ride him, take his seed
...and his soul.

~

Cheyenne McCray
(author of the Riding Tall and Rough & Ready series)
Love is Strange: Tales of Paranormal Passion

SHIT AND YOU

{this poem does not follow the book's sexual theme.
but I like the piece too much to push it aside.
therefore I'll share its vulgarity}

you too
cling to my insides
the remains of things once
         all the good is gone
it's more than
         the milky brown tone
sticking you and shit
         in a category
              all your own

you too
     choked my spirit
     as I pushed you away
              persistently
fighting endlessly
the inevitable separation
         of you and me

I knew
there was little substance left
tight was your hold on me
         as I prayed for you to let go
unwilling to accept your destiny
     to be dumped
        and move on in the waters
                 waiting below

and I knew
sooner than later
         your grip would slip
and you'd release
         my churning hips

of you, I'd finally be free
and you'd be free of me

seems we knew
it would soon be over
    when I swallowed
      your candy-coated bullshit

we knew
    this union couldn't last long
'cause there was
    some good stuff
      about you
but some other shit
that I couldn't deal wit'
    was severely wrong

so our relationship
    would soon disperse
you gave me a hard time
    but you weren't the first

    now I, too
    think of you
whenever
    my anus starts to eclipse
    and a sweat rises above my lips
whenever
    I must sit
    upon the porcelain throne
      a little too long

I think about you
whenever
    I'm struggling and time
      seems to pass slow

I think about you
whenever
    I'm having a hard time
    trying to let some trifling shit go

    there are days
when shit and you are similar
    in so many ways

**I WOULDN'T SUCK
YOUR LOUSY DICK
IF I WAS SUFFOCATING
AND
THERE WAS OXYGEN
IN YOUR BALLS**

~

**Taffy Davenport
(Mink Stole)**
(actress, singer, attitude)
Female Trouble, 1975

Predator

how many souls have you devoured
to appease the appetite of your ravenous ego

how many borders have you crossed
hearts have you broken/dismantled
shattered into unidentifiable chunks
of suddenly needless flesh

how many women have loved you
given their best
yet nothing was returned

when will you be satisfied
when will you stop tossing them aside

will it take a voicemail from a victim
living in hell/ready to die

no longer inspired
after she begged and cried
forgot spirit was her guide
'cause you temporarily admired
constantly lied

now she sits on the roadside
gun on the passenger seat of her ride
screaming "i'm tired, i'm tired"

selfishly victimizing another person
{taking body, teasing mind, contaminating spirit}
has to be the lowest form
of human exploitation
such primitive and narcissistic behavior

~
Curv Brown
(possessor of a patchwork heart)

Dicktionary

alimony
    the screwing you get for the screwing you got
                                                 ~ graffiti

beauty
    the power by which a woman
    charms a lover and terrifies a husband
                     ~ Ambrose Bierce (editorialist, satirist)

brain
    viewed as an appendage of the genital glands
                 ~ Carl Jung (founder of analytical psychology)

closet
    a terrible place to die
                                                 ~ graffiti

easy
    an adjective used to describe
    a woman who has the sexual morals of a man
                             ~ Nancy Linn-Desmond (author)

experience
    the name everybody gives to their mistakes
                             ~ Oscar Wilde (playwright, poet)

gentleman
    a patient wolf
                     ~ Henrietta Tiarks (Duchess, fashion model)

homosexuality
    a pain in the ass
                                                 ~ graffiti

liberated woman
one who has sex before marriage and a job after
~ Gloria Steinem (women's rights advocate)

love
the irresistible desire to be irresistibly desired
~ Robert Frost (Pulitzer Prize winning poet)

masturbation
the primary sexual activity of mankind
in the 19th century, it was a disease;
in the 20th, it's a cure
~ Thomas Szasz (psychiatrist, academic)

nymphomaniac
a woman as obsessed with sex as an average man
~ Mignon McLaughlin (journalist, author)

perfect lover
one who turns into a pizza at 4:00 AM
~ Charles Pierce (female impressionist)

platonic relationship
the interval between
the introduction and the first kiss
~ Sophie Irene Loeb (social-welfare advocate)

promiscuous person
someone who is getting more sex than you are
~ Victor Lownes (Playboy magazine executive)

sex
the thing that takes up the least amount of time
and causes the most amount of trouble
~ John Barrymore (actor, Drew's grandfather)

Chapter 4

Southern Comfort

Threesomes with Me, Myself, & I

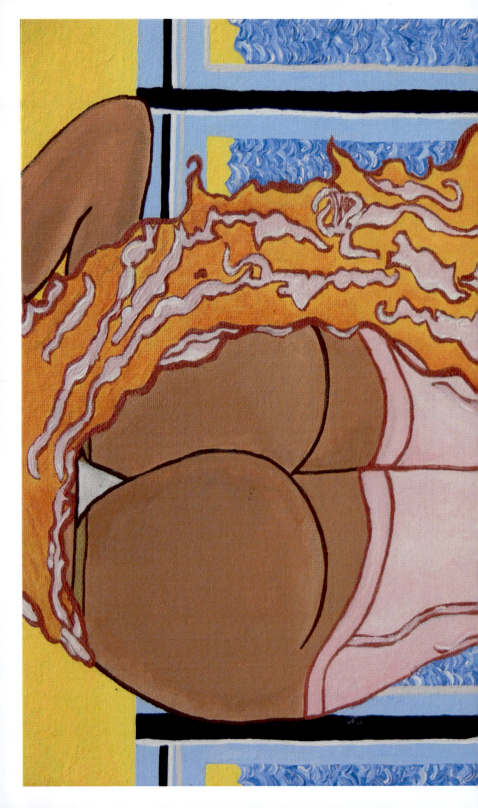

Monkey's Demands

baby, i swear
    tonight i rushed
        i left work on time
      darted thru traffic
          as if i'd lost my mind

selected my outfit quickly
      showered swiftly
applied make-up
    with a sweeping stride
only once
    did i lotion my backside
        'cause i was rushing

    i was determined
          to be on time
and sex was the farthest thing
        from my mind

i couldn't allow
    its undeniable delectability
      to derail my punctuality
        when in all actuality
i just wanted to be with you, my loverman
      so i focused on the minute hand

but when i entered the bedroom
          to grab my purse
out of the blue
    started the monkey's curse

the rumpled sheets caught my eye
         and i can't lie
i couldn't stop
    thinking of last night
    thinking of you
the smell of sweet sweat
all sticky wet
    when we were thru

suddenly
on my back
    raged a monkey
        seeking an orgasmic prize
it kept tossing images
   at my forehead
      landing lightly
         at the meeting of my thighs
although the monkey's presence
         my watch despised

    there was no room for choice
my body had to obey
   that fucking monkey's voice

so in an effort
   to shave minutes
      from my certain delay
    i hurried
      the primate on its way
i dropped my pants
      to my knees
to quickly address
    the monkey's needs

i turned on the vibrator
        in a single twist
and allowed its pulsation
     to give my clit a kiss

darling, i don't think you understand
      i fucked myself standing up
        so i could hurry up
and meet that monkey's demands

         it was my intent
that my late arrival you wouldn't resent

   so i focused
     on one of our freakier events
don't you remember last night
when we gave new life to an old position

when you smacked me on my ass
   and asked "now, do I have
     your full fucking undivided attention"
when I crowned you my king
     and you labeled me your ho
as we laid breathless happy
      in a unifying glow

baby don't banish me as guilty
      for i shall acquit
only my climax
   would ease the monkey's horny fit
the magic wand rocked
    back and forth but would not quit
'cause there was a nut
   somewhere in me
     that my monkey had to get

baby, i apologize
  if my rationalization
    is causing irritation
   i tried to oblige/expeditiously
so please, don't blame
   this whole thing...on me

i had to have you
      right there, right then
i just did my fucking best
   to bring its antics to an end

besides it started the whole mess
riding my ass
   allowing my mind no rest
until my clit
   found a throbbing happiness

please don't blame me
   for a tardy i couldn't prevent
if you plan on being pissed off
   it's my fucking monkey
     you ought to resent

Speak To Your Freak
(Quickie Questionnaire for your Derriere)

what is your preferred
sexual position

do you enjoy making love with
a moaner or a wailer

which lover
has the greatest hand job

are you sexually active

are you having safe sex

have you been tested
in last 6 months

who is your
a) favorite fucker
b) sweetest toucher
c) best kisser
d) most romantic lover

are you dominant or submissive

what is the longest time
you've had sex
with someone

in what forbidden place
do you wish to have sex

what is the longest time
you've had sex
with yourself

do you
use pornography
{ what kind appeals to you }

do you practice tantric sex
or wish you knew how

which lover
has the greatest lip services
(upper body and lower body)

are you
an exhibitionist or a voyeur

do you enjoy making love with
a quiet cummer
or an animated screamer

(see, hear, taste, smell, touch)
what sense moves you most?

do you enjoy anal sex
< watching, giving, receiving >

Six Senses {ESP}

Claire's Voyance

call it what you will
but she knows how she feels

woman's intuition
psychic telepathy
something told her
to question your loyalty

standing on the back of her neck
were alarms in the form of fine hair
there was an exotic stench
augmenting Claire's air

minor alterations
to your routine course
delayed response followed
by a crackle in your voice

chill in your fingers
replaced the red-hot bliss
as your ashy lips cooled her cheeks
with the frost of your kiss

bizarre demonic distance
in the pits of your eyes
something told her
you are telling a bunch of lies

call it what you will
but after you left
something told Claire
she was better off by her damn self

Quoteworthy: The Unknown

When a person has sex,
they're having it with everybody
that partner has had it with
for the past ten years.

~

Otis Ray Bowen
(US Secretary of Health and Human Services)

There is hardly anyone whose sexual life,
if it were broadcast,
would not fill the world at large
with surprise and horror

~

William Somerset Maugham
(British playwright, novelist)

For the first time in history,
sex is more dangerous
than the cigarette afterward

~

Jay Leno
(Television host, stand-up comedian)

Piping Hot

current location and clothing
    were forevermore irrelevant
even over the phone
    he knew how to turn me on

        thong, g-string, or cotton-free
it mattered not if I was stuck in traffic
    or had a vibrator buzzing next to me

his lustful lips showed no concern
    whether I was naked
        or my shoulders were draped
his mouth
    lustfully babbled
        as his scandalous thoughts escaped

he was always saying something nasty
    my coochie could appreciate
requiring that my mind, body, and soul
        participate
the greatest impact
    was made by his voice
        although he did not say a lot
one time he came
    out of left field
        making a statement I never forgot
steamed up my phone
    as I drove home
        treated me like a deadpan sexpot
how dare him
    place pressure on a nut I've yet got
    when he said
        "do, baby, remember me
        the next time
        your pussy is piping hot"

    shocked to silence, I remain
    never to picture him the same

        thus begun my mad dash home
I needed
        about fifteen solid minutes...alone

errands were rescheduled
        I had to get there quick

I needed some loving
        even if it was electric
but
little was required
        given the vivid visions
                I still had of his dick

he played the leading role
        in my imaginary plot
sweat had no time to pour
        bam...my body rapidly shot
responding eagerly
        (like the last time
                he rubbed my g-spot)
though he was absent
        his memoirs stirred my honey pot
echoes of words just heard
left my she steaming from his memory
                while piping hot

♥♥♥♥♥♥♥
WHAT DO ATHEISTS
SCREAM
when they come
?

~

Bill Hicks
(stand-up comedian, satirist)

THE MAN IN ME | MENTALLY

quiet
reserved
      unaware
calm
comfort
    you sat there

               silently
your body was screaming to me

pheromones were rising
from the depths
        of your buxom chest
you, being a diligent lover
would settle only
      for the title of best

    without a single word
your capabilities were heard

in the presence of your quietness
      I constructed another scenery
you shall be the damsel distressed
      in my very next sexual fantasy

you didn't know
      I'd dare not say verbally
but after while
      you gon be fucking me

I'll visualize your nudity
        after you go home
your memory will gently glide
      up and down my sexbone

as you sit before me
        clothed and content

my dick hardens secretly
              with no merciful intent

though your reasoning
for not being lovers
              I fully understand
logic don't stop the urge
to shove my hand
              into your pants
so I'll back off
discontinue my pursuit
           and respect your wish
but my dick is mad
protesting
      with a clenched raised fist

keep that juicy ass
all to yourself
          let me not swim in your cherry sea
because later on
after you go home
       I'm gon fuck the shit out of you mentally 👄

terms every porn consumer should know

The Cumaway

The cutaway shot
of a man's face as he cums.
After the actual pop shot,
it's the most important thing
you'll film all day.

~

Seth Grahame-Smith
(author, screenwriter, producer)
The Big Book of Porn:
A Penetrating Look at the World of Dirty Movies

Filthy 5-Letter Favorites: DILDO

Bob intimidates most men

initially, viewed as a cheap date

a short-lived necessity

a means to eliminate Miss Laycock's misery

a quencher for her masturbational urge
when companions left her starving
for orgasms

Bob
battery ✺ operated ✺ boyfriend
was never intended
for a long-term relationship

not originally purchased as a commitment

out of the blue, she found herself dependent
on his predictable erection

she thought he'd service her for a season

a temporary synthetic employee
who would occasionally fill in
for that third leg
she was missing

now, a decade later
Bob is her plastic pimp

pushing her buttons left barren
by lovers long gone

providing his mechanical touch
in the midst of
her murky dickless nights

Her Little Black Dildo

long for the touch of muscles
                covered by colored flesh
dream of penetration
       a sturdy rod bringing her happiness

in the meantime
      alone she shower
      alone she undress
          and she's okay with this aloneliness
until her marriage is resolved
    (and she can fuck guilt-free)
            she must accept second best

with the dildo's vibrating motion
                her clit she'll caress
smooth plastic, two batteries
           to fill her emptiness

dipped in love juice
      bathed in her honey's milkiness
it makes her toes curl
      relieves tension and relaxes stress

and maintains her feeling
             of loyalness
while making her whisper
        "yes, yes, yes"

♥♥♥♥♥♥

if masturbating was a crime,
how quickly would you be arrested?
personally, I'd hide out
with a vibrator and a big box of batteries
then voluntarily turn myself in
next week

~

Curv Brown
(my own all-time greatest lover)

THE MAN IN ME | GIRL OF MY DREAMS

good looking plus great fucking

to screw me, she need not be near
she fucks me
        even when she's not here

my middle leg has been spoiled
                my mind is blown
I think of her whenever
      I have a pleasurable moment alone

I'd dare not mess around
              never take her for granted
to possess her heart
        gives me an exclusive advantage

for my lover defies the norm
              she's worth her weight in gold
'cause she swallows me whole
                  while touching my soul

I love her hands, her mounds, her mouth
from her ambitious mind to her sticky south

reminiscing on our rendezvous comes easy
her loving's satisfying, tantalizing, and sleazy

during those times
      when I'm on the edge
           of spewing my lava
                till nothing is left
      my mind gravitates
                      to no one else
for she's the girl of my dreams
                when I touch myself

Fucking For One:
Masturbational Matching

1) five finger
2) tiptoe through
3) unload
4) polish
5) harass
6) spank
7) shake
8) Jack
9) diddle
10) shifting
11) hand
12) airing
13) Jillin'
14) dip
15) making
16) paint
17) hold
18) pedicure
19) dropping the kids
20) beef
21) go knuckle

A) the ceiling
B) the Skittles
C) the camel toes
D) Off
E) humpin'
F) off at the pool
G) soup
H) the pistol
I) the creamer
J) the milkman
K) strokin'-off
L) the sausage hostage
M) the two lips
N) the pearl
O) the beanstock
P) the orchid
Q) the monkey
R) shuffle
S) deep
T) the manual transmission
U) the digits

Answers: 1) R, 2) M, 3) H, 4) N, 5) J, 6) Q, 7) I, 8) O, 9) B, 10) T, 11) E, 12) P, 13) D, 14) U, 15) G, 16) A, 17) L, 18) C, 19) F, 20) K, 21) S

Sticky Fingers

i promise to tell the truth, the whole truth
        and nothing but my truth
yes, ladies and gentlemen of the court
i've been charged with robbery
        armed sexual robbery

i can't fully explain why i did it
        sad to admit it
this wasn't the first time
        and it probably won't be the last
    for some strange reasons
   during these horny seasons
        i can't stop touching my own ass
it's just this time, i got caught

a kleptomaniac when it comes to my clit
   i go unconscious
   wake up and find myself rubbing it

try as i may
   to keep my hands off of good things
        my will can't resist
the stimulating satisfaction
        found in my fingertip's bliss
   during those lonely interludes
   when my body takes out the time
        to give herself a kiss

how can i be expected
   with such erotic expertise
        to control my insatiable spirit
i get off on the sound of my own name
   even if occasionally
        i have to use my own lips to hear it
but you
   the jurors
    who have been chosen to judge me
      are all more civilized

when it comes to the taming
of your sexuality
so please have a little sympathy
for a woman suffering
with self-sufficient disability
because i am possessed
by an unquenchable spirit
and the prosecutor's 4 experts
couldn't explain it
and testimonies
by a trail of my past lovers
have proven that some of the best of men
couldn't tame it
so i can only hope
that you will forgive me
for this masturbational crime
just one more time
do keep in mind
that my actions were mostly involuntary

'cause i was born handi-capable
i came into this world
a lioness of lustfulness
a manifestation
straight from the pages of Sigmund Freud
i am that sexual savage
whom weak men should avoid
i'm the animal who cracks all the nuts
others refuse to give away
so i'm begging, i'm pleading
for your forgiveness today

honestly
i believe the government
is supporting this conspiracy
sending their detectives
with cameras and baggies
to collect my privacy
then toss them on this table
for all the world to see
oh, i deserve time served

                        after what they did to me
i was ten seconds
        from an orgasm
                when the po-po
                kicked in my front door
and the boys in blue
                instantly labeled me a whore
they snatched up my hot ass
        off those warm sheets
        and carted me to a cold cell
        in a place i ain't never been before

there were
mug shots, fingerprints,
        cold grits, and orange jumpsuits
for masturbation
i was caged
        with smugglers, robbers,
                addicts, and prostitutes

and still i don't know why
                i can't be left alone
why is it against the law
        for me to comfort myself
        in the comforts of my own home

yes, your honor
and distinguished members of this jury
        i realize the evidence
                is mounded against me

exhibit #1
a baggie of my rumpled sheets
        encasing the composure
        of this curvature
                        upon further review
                        revealed a spot or two
                later identified as cum residue

then there's **exhibit #2**
my vibrator
        though still warm,

            it was smoking when found
and when they hauled it off
to the lab, the batteries tested
                        way, way down

which to some, may seem to prove
                              frequent use
         but to others
            it could be misinterpreted as abuse

i can't deny it
   i know i have an issue
       for which there seems no cure
and though
      this ass may be filthy
              my heart remains pure
but i just can't see
            how imprisoning me
         is going to stop this urgency
              to play with my punany

therefore
i throw myself
on the mercy of the court
             and implore your deepest empathy
   as you deliberate the sexual sentencing
             for the assault of myself by me
'cause once again
       as you can see
          on this photo
             marked **exhibit #3**
                          i've been caught
                       with sticky fingers   👄

STOP TOUCHING YOURSELF

•••

we have a guest!

~

The Schizo Girl
(Penny Flame)
(model, adult film actor, producer)
Repo Girl, 2003

Quoteworthy: Education

You cannot have sex education
without saying that sex is natural
and that most people find it pleasurable

~

Bruno Bettelheim
(Austrian child psychologist with a Freudian focus)

(regarding masturbation)
I think that it is something
that's part of human sexuality
and it's part of something
that perhaps should be taught

but we've not even taught
our children the very basics

and I feel
that we have tried ignorance
for a very long time
and it's time we try
education

~

Dr. Joycelyn Elders
(educator, pediatrician, Surgeon General)

Do you know...
THE SEX HOLIDAYS

<u>National Condom Month</u>
<u>Anal Sex Month</u>
February

Annual Threesome Day – **March 3rd**
Steak & Blow Job Day – **March 14th**
National Lingerie Day – **April 24th**
National Outdoor Intercourse Day – **May 8th**
National Sex Day – **May 25th**
National Masturbation Day – **May 28th**

<u>LGBTQ Pride Month</u>
June

National Lollipop Day – **July 20th**

<u>Breast Health Awareness Month</u>
<u>LGBT History Month</u>
October

National Coming Out Day – **October 11th**
International Fisting Day – **October 21st**
Sex Toy Day – **November 8th**

Freaky Aphrodisiacs
FOODS THAT SEXUALLY MOTIVATE

almonds, pine nuts, walnuts

avocado

bananas

cherries and grapes

chili peppers

chocolate and truffles

chai tea and coffee

ginger, ginseng, licorice

olive oil

pineapple

pomegranates

oysters, salmon, lobster, shrimp, mussel

strawberries

watermelon

Curv Cummentary

Recommendation For Masturbation

"I see the sexually miserable everywhere"

When I think of the orgasmically-deprived, no single image comes to mind. Daily, I encounter a variety of people suffering from a lack of love. They are famished for stimulation.

regardless of companionship,
I must ask the sexually sad,
why do you
deprive yourself
of physical pleasure?

The care of your temple goes beyond flossing teeth and keeping your crevices clean. To ensure well-being, you must do more than exercise and eat more vegetables. I urge you to be accepting of your body's necessities (if they don't involve or envision another person being harmed).

masturbate

• origin: Latin *manus* (hand) and *turbare* (to disturb) •

to shift your own gears, to read your body's Braille
to butter your biscuit, to ring your own bell

There's nothing wrong with lending yourself a helping hand. Self-Sexual-Assistance (SSA equals ASS backwards) has perks that go beyond its shivers. I encourage you to seek this liberation. Personally, I place orgasms on my priority list just below life insurance.

The 4 Benefits of Getting Yourself Off

STRESS-RELIEF: When your body has a convulsion of bliss and you feel the free-flowing of cream, there's a shift of hormones. Instantly, you feel better and less tense. Plus, there's a bonus. Try masturbating until you break a sweat.

>   you can burn a few calories
>   during the process

ECONOMICAL: If you are an auto-masochist (capable of busting a nut by merely using your hand), your orgasms are free. For those "technologically orgasmic" (needing a toy or tool), your pleasure cums at a low price with a low maintenance charge (batteries). Either way in the end, you get your rocks off and

>   self-satisfaction remains a bargain

CREATIVITY: Southern Comfort requires concentration and imagination. As a masturbator, you must know what it takes to stimulate yourself sexually. Then use that knowledge to coach yourself mentally while arousing yourself physically. Masturbation is your blank canvas. Even if you are a guy using a flick while choking your dick,

>   you have to envision yourself in the act
>   what is your favorite role?
>   voyeur, fucker, or director

DISEASE-FREE: In your mind, you can go back to the days of free love ~ fucking without a glove. My abstinence motto is

> i never worry about an STD
> from myself and I screwing me

Solo sex is mostly mental. But in order to do it correctly, it requires acceptance of who you are and honesty about what you like. In closing,

You must take care of *You*

♥ ♥ ♥ ♥ ♥ ♥ ♥

remember to pacify
your sexual passions

♥ ♥ ♥ ♥ ♥ ♥ ♥ ♥

To Love Oneself
is the beginning
of a lifelong romance

~

Oscar Wilde
(Irish author, playwright, poet)

Keep Touching Me

you touch me in my dreams

your glazed strokes
sweep across
    my budding clitoris
        pressing down
           encouraging its enlargement

your licked fondles
squeeze about
    my thickening tips
        encircling the circumference
           building their bulge

my imitation wand
starts on low
    slowly rubbing
        across my lips
        occasionally concentrating
                at my apex

as my nipples stiffen
under its shaking clutch
    as the pulsating speed increases
            focusing on my climax

I shiver from a relieving explosion

when my legs stop shaking
        its vibrations cease
my lips wet
        my mind at peace

slowly I cover my body
sleepily I close my eyes

promptly I fall asleep
        continuing
        my dreams of you

Bed Besieged By Brothers

girlfriend
your typical masturbation imagery
consist of one lucky individual

usually no face
bulging triceps and biceps
a nice thick ass
powering one outstanding muscle

sometimes
you're an exhibitionist
he sits at the foot of your bed
      watching you please yourself

periodically
you prefer the exotic
      there are two (or three) mysterious men
most times, they pleasure you
other times, you please them

today your realm expanded

as you closed your eyes
to fantasize of your approaching orgasm
a large crowd of mysterious men
gradually encircled your bed
making the exotic exhibitionist
within you
      ecstatically happy

but when the pulsations paused
you began contemplating

      "were they previous lovers?"

you couldn't foresee
this vision manifesting

how could you find enchantment
ass out
before a gathering of faceless men

perhaps
Spirit was showing you
the infinite possibilities

perhaps
you should be
questioning
your continual self-pleasing
     with various plastics
         and penis-substituting fingers
while a Universe of gorgeous beings
    bearing bona-fide bones
       wait to assist you
       want to assist you   

**a man can sleep around,
no questions asked**

**but if a woman makes
19 or 20
mistakes,
she's a tramp**

~

Joan Rivers
(comedian, talk show host)

Warm Honey Awaits You

maybe this time
she'll be honest
    tell you how she was just amusing herself
    tell you
    of your magnificent mental performance
    tell you she's holding the phone
    with her left hand ... for a reason

holding the receiver snug...
    waiting
    silently impatiently
    waiting
holding onto each breath
    (hers and yours)
    as the conversation
        starts staggering

hoping your next sentence
    will be in the form of a question
    inquiring about this evening's plans

so she begs of you quietly
    part your deliciously juicy lips
    lower the tone of your voice
    ask her
        "what are you doing tonight"

this time
    she'll stop trying to
        unconsciously calculate
        how long she's known you
        how many times you've dined
        how often you call

when you pose the question
    she'll be honest
    smooth shall be the delivery
        of her anticipated response

honey-licking your ear

ask her
    "what are you doing tonight"

and she'll reply
    "I'm doing whatever you want me to"

ask her

ask her

    cum on
        just
        ask her
            'cause you know
        her answer will be...yes

I'd like to see
the sexual activity
of one fellow I know
because
he's an
energetic,
sophisticated whore
with the tongue of a lion
& the dick of a donkey

so naturally,
he peaks my curiosity

~

Curv Brown
(phenomenal poem crusher)

Nutless

i can't press my spine
into these silky soft sheets
nor can i overlook the buzz's moving tone
with its pumping being impelled
by the last of this evening's energy

my rest refuses to welcome me
soaked in a soggy creaminess
of instigated seduction

low on steam and tenacity

my exhaustion requires refueling

slowly i go to sleep/drained and dry

Six Senses {TOUCH}

doing herself

"looking well-lubed and frequently ridden"

Constantly having to touch herself,
she worries about the absence of a man.
Is her best seed being wasted,
harvested by her oh-too-capable hand?
Will this perfected practice
of polishing the family jewels
keep her next lover at bay
because her face is silently testifying
she's been fucked today?

*the only thing
I regret
about my past
is the length of it*

*if I had to live
my life again,
I'd make
all
the same mistakes
. . .
only sooner*

~

Tallulah Bankhead
(flamboyant, award winning screen actress)

Two One-Night Stands

hear ye, hear ye
this weekend
somebodies gone to get a piece of me
this weekend
some cuties gonna get lucky
     'cause I'm hot with plenty of booty

    I'm tired of taking matters into my own hands
        I need a man (or two)
   to kiss me, hold me, do the physical moves
        I've been longing to do

    making a second nighter not good enough
      for two nights I want only fresh stuff
    only rested lap rockets allowed in sockets

in place of doodling with a dildo
        a man from my past
       shall tap this ass
    and another man brand new
      shall get some too

it matters not
if this is trampish behavior
       my scandalous weekend
     shall be between me, he, and he
      until I call my main girls up
       adding she and she
     explaining my lustful logic
    comparing each man's ingenuity

just as sure as today is Friday
there are two male replacements
    pre-destined to enjoy me tomorrow
                 and tonight
but only
    if they are full of energy
       down for whatever
             and acting right

in a couple of hours, I shall dwell
                    in love's hypnotic relief
    as they unknowingly
                    take turns sharing their beef

I've been more than patient
        pouring my passions upon my fake flesh toy
        waiting for the chance to cradle a real boy

I've tired of solo sex
twirling pearl > beating the beaver
            making the kitty purr > reading Braille
fanning the furnace > scuffing the muffin
        finger dancing > ringing the southern belle

this weekend, there will be man1 and man2
            no petal pushing or unplugging the drain
because technological orgasms
                have finally driven me insane

my booty calls are confirmed
    and each man thinks he's the only one
I have no intention of deceiving them
        I just need to have some real fucking fun

Hey baby what is your problem?
Huh, you got a problem?
You're good looking,
you got a beautiful body,
beautiful legs, beautiful face,
all these guys in love with you.
Only you got a look in your eye
like you haven't been fucked in a year!

~

Tony Montana
(Al Pacino)
(film and stage actor, director)
Scarface, 1983

Sight Unseen

abundance of cerebral agility
          surrounds her
the foggy dark utopia
        starts here

after showing her
      the mind-numbing heights of higher ecstasy
      you've been crowned her ultimate fantasy

mentally, right now
you enfold her limbs
into contortionist disfigurements
that her closest friends wouldn't believe
          she could achieve

     you, the pretzel-maker/her, the dough
    molded by one mastering elation's ebb and flow

this is where it all emerges

mentally, right now
    as you tenderize
        the cellulite padding
        her inner thighs
            accepting your use
                  of penile power
she refers only to you
          in this hallucinating hour

the king of her castle
the emperor of her intimate infatuations
the receiver of her public displays of affection
      affirming to passersby
      that you've fucked, are fucking,
              and shall fuck some more
        for you, she is naughtily willing to explore

remembrance of your scent
      ignites a horny yearning

that sparkles the fuel
    dousing her flaming coals

thoughts of you
illuminate her rosy reproduction
    in self-directing screenplays

your past interactions
causing multiple reactions
    as she masturbates
        behind your back
            ...and dreams you were there 👄

❤❤❤❤❤❤❤

**Books are finite,
sexual encounters are finite,
but the desire to read
and to fuck
is infinite;
it surpasses our own deaths,
our fears,
our hopes for peace.**

~

Roberto Bolano
(Chilean novelist, poet)

Bona Fide Sex

This evening I held a dick
In the palm of my hand
There was no body present
It didn't belong to a man

It's been a long time
Since I saw one not in print or on film
I've grown anxious, obviously desperate
For one connected to a "him"

When I purchased this cock earlier today
I stood at the register in shame
Premeditating this acquisition
I stopped for cash
So they wouldn't know my name

The male attendant stared into my face
With a deliberately discomforting grin
Put batteries in my selection, turned it on
Thinking of what I would soon put it in

This constant craving embarrassed me
My overpowering need for such an artificial thing
A restless, horny fiend
Trying to focus on the joy it would bring

But its beauty and structure
Caused me to sit still, reflect
Think of some of the real ones
I have held with the highest respect

Adoration for their power
Thrust and sense of duty
Thankful for the satisfaction
They have brought to this booty

Some were beautiful, unforgettable
Solid, straight, even in tone

Some were multihued, others curved
From short and medium to extra long

I've learned that size doesn't matter
But dexterity makes the man
Most have learned to work what they have
Others do the best they can

My secret collection of plastic joy
Escalates my lonesome fears
As I bring myself pleasure
It occasionally drives me to tears

I want a man to suck my nipples
Strong hands to rub my back
A man with a God-given penis
Able to alleviate my lack

I want passion and breath and moans
Sweat with a manly scent
I want a dick with a body
Without guilt and everlasting resent

Maybe this is a moment in my time
A pacifier to hold me over
But I long for a man to part my thighs
And tell my dildo to move over

VAGINAL MUSCLES

are your love muscles
and should be exercised
along with the rest of the body

~

Anne Hooper
(writer, researcher, therapist)

Curv Cummentary

Good Vibrations
Purchasing The Perfect Penis

This is an article for the "believe-in-fucking" folks, who are contemplating the purchase of an energized sexual aid. It is a cummentary intended to be a guide for the vibration virgins and a review for the stirred-and-shaken veterans. I hope you enjoy this informative interruption in the midst of my poetry.

prior to any purchase,
take the time to consider
the penile characteristics you prefer

In order to fully utilize this insert, you will have to be a bit selfish. For a moment, you must think of what you enjoy. {Or, if you're buying a bone for a lover, you must reflect on their shared fantasies and the touch they've responded to sexually.} For a moment, you have to be mindful of what satisfies the recipient of the vibrator's vibrations.

DON'T WASTE YOUR MONEY, HONEY
☺ **you can't cum right**
with the wrong dick ☹

I have bought incompatible plastic lovers on several occasions. Purchased penises too large for recurring use and too veiny for easy penetration. Some made of the wrong material even caused irritation. Others had vibrations in the wrong area. So take your time. Calm down long enough to think of your deepest desires.

what kind of lover toy
could you personally enjoy

A few considerations have been listed to help you make the best possible selection. Let's get started...

size
▶ what size would you like? length and width? ◀

The range of sizes available stretches from as small as a fingertip to larger than an "11 inches of hardcore punishment" Lexington Steele replica (www.lexsteele.com). Think of the dick size you enjoy. Now ask yourself: would you like one compact in size and no hassle to hide, medium in mass and mobile, or outsized and beckoning for the spotlight? Take the time to evaluate or you are bound to buy the wrong thing. And remember:

just like grocery shopping while hungry,
you shouldn't purchase a penis while horny

vibration
▶ what area do you like to feel gyrating? ◀

Consider the type of vibration you enjoy. Generally, a vibrator's mechanism is in the base or at the tip. If the penis substitute will be solely used for rim stimulation, consider a base vibration. This will place the throb at the brim of your opening when the "Johnny-on-the-spot" is fully inserted. If you enjoy clitoral, cervical, G-spot, or P-spot (prostrate) stimulation, you may prefer a vibrator with its power in the tip. There are also dual- and triple-action vibrators like the Jack Rabbit. However, if this is your first,

start with something simple.
you can buy something more complex and costly next time.

power
▶ how will this vibe be electrified? ◀

Envision your power source. Battery or electric? I haven't seen a solar-powered one. But please consider rechargeable batteries. Keep in mind that most of the time

...the bigger the battery, the louder the buzz.

shape
▶ what structure is most stimulating? ◀

You must contemplate its shape once you decide on size and area of pulse. What would you like to feel? ▶ Do you want a straight vibrator or a curved one targeting your G-spot? ▶ Do you want your

B.O.B. (battery operated boyfriend) to look like a penis? With or without veins? With or without a defined tip? With or without testicles? ▶ Would you prefer one with a manufactured pattern? Vertical or horizontal? Waves, ridges, or swirls? What would you like?

material
▶ what feeling would your privates prefer? ◀

(I) Phallic substitutes are commonly categorized as hard plastic or silicone. (II) The hard types are solid in structure and inflexible. If there is a small nick or ridge on the piece, you may salvage it with a nail file depending on the material. If it can't be simply repaired, it should be replaced. (III) Silicone stand-ins come in a variety of textures from flesh-imitation to jelly-filled. Along with its cushioned exterior, there may also be flexibility.

Always use a condom,
especially on those feeling like a real penis.

color
▶ what tone turns you on? ◀

The pigment of a plastic poker comes in a range of shades from primary colors to flesh tones. Choice of hue is up to you.

where to buy
▶ you have a few options ◀

Some companies will send you a catalog in a brown paper bag wrapper. Mail the insert or purchase over the phone. The internet gives you the most options with its international connections, taking you to numerous locations at the click of your mouse. However you may want to see the sex toy in person so a sex shop is the perfect solution. If you want to protect your right to privacy, call ahead (just block your number before dialing) and verify that they carry the delight that you found on the internet. Visit the location late at night, allowing the cloak of darkness to conceal your identity.

Be sure to pay with cash
so they can never trace that fake dick back to your ass.

These helpful hints will aid you in your purchasing of a piece for your peace. If you really like the vibrator, be sure to write down the details (manufacturer, model #, where to purchase) and keep this data in an important place. It could come in handy when the time comes for a replacement. But stay open minded because vibrators change like fashion, here today, gone tomorrow. So don't become dependent on a specified type.

mechanical loving:
NEED-TO-KNOWS

0 clean your vibrator after every use.
yes, dear...you can give yourself an infection with a fake erection. there are special cleansers available, gentle and powerful enough so your toy isn't damaged. but do not submerge a vibrator in water unless it is waterproof.

0 use a condom with all vibrators, especially jelly-filled or flesh-imitating vibrators.
their plastic may contain phthalates and the surface of these softer selections will break down over time. thus, exposing the user to toxins. it may seem like an inconvenience but please protect yourself while pleasing yourself.

0 use a water-based lubricant.
this will allow for friction free insertion. you don't want to damage the family jewels while jilling off.

0 be considerate of your partner.
if you have a partner with an attached penis, please be considerate. i would suggest starting with a Bob (battery operated boyfriend) smaller than their piece (unless they suggest differently). if you have a partner who is gone for extensive periods of time, discontinue all use at least 7 days before their return and do Kegel exercises. never allow your plastic penetrator to mess up your connection to a real dick.

make love to yourself
to the best of your ability

STIMULATING WEBSITES

I've always been inquisitive. My determination to better sexually educate myself has led to the discovery of some very informative sites on the internet. May they assist you in your quest for increased pleasure.

www.a-womans-touch.com
A boutique dedicated to providing information about sexual health, education, and healthy pleasure. This is a sexuality resource center offering extensive informative articles.

www.tenga-global.com
"A Revolution in Male Pleasure." They provide a wide array of sexual stimulators exclusively for men. Products offered are impressive because they accommodate such a wide spectrum of pleasurables.

www.babeland.com
This site has the best toy reviews. For each vibrator, it provides thorough descriptions, including the type of material, size (both length and girth), batteries needed, intensity of vibration, and volume. Plus, it instructs you on "how to find your g-spot". A great variety of sex toy kits.

www.comeasyouare.com
Here you will find step-by-step instructions on "how to use a vibrator." Also this site has shopping guides providing a sound level rating for each vibrator in its description.

www.goodvibes.com
A good detailed site. Its data is very extensive. Weekly articles and blogs are impressive. Plus, the items offered are phthalates-free and all have reviews and ratings.

www.kegel-exercises.com
Ladies and Gentlemen, do your Kegel exercises! Keep your stuff tight. Review this site for detailed instructions to track your progress. They also offer a Prostate Massager and Kegel weights.

www.libida.com
Chock-full of information. Categories like tips and techniques, health and info, beyond toys, and erotic stories are included on the site. Wonderful layout provides easy navigation.

seek answers for your sexual questions, just like anything else affecting your health

extra! extra!

If you don't desire
the rhythm and racket
of a vibrator,

try a dildo

(a plastic penis
with no power)

they tend to be
less expensive
since there isn't
a motor implanted

love yourself

do yourself

In closing,
I encourage you to
pamper yourself
frequently

and sex yourself
whenever necessary

remember:
you must love you
FIRST

THE MONEY SHOT

let my words

urge every reader

to relax

❥

to laugh

❥

to love

❥

to fuck

RESPONSIBLY

Truly,

Curv Brown

everybody should cum ♥ everybody should cum

Recommended Reading

69 Ways To Please Your Lover:
Sex Secrets for Ultimate Pleasure
Nicole Bailey
★📖★

The Encyclopedia of Sacred Sexuality
from Aphrodisiacs and Ecstasy
to Yoni Worship and Zap-lam Yoga
Rufus C. Camphausen
★📖★

Satisfaction: The Art of the Female Orgasm
Kim Cattrall and Mark Levinson
★📖★

The Complete Illustrated Kama Sutra
Edited by Lance Dane
★📖★

XXX Sex...Tonight!
Anne Hooper
★📖★

The Wild Guide to Sex and Loving
Siobhan Kelly
★📖★

Dark Eros : Black Erotic Writings
Edited by Reginald Martin
★📖★

Will the Real Women...Please Stand Up!
Uncommon Sense about Sex, Sensuality, and Self-Discovery
Ella Patterson
★📖★

I Love Female Orgasm: An Extraordinary Orgasm Guide
Dorian Solot and Marshall Miller
★📖★

Rec Sex: An A-Z Guide to Hooking Up
Em and Lo (Emma Taylor and Lorelei Sharkey)

ABOUT THE AUTHOR

Curv **Brown**

is an erotic scholar.
Born and residing in Atlanta.
This is her first full-length book
of many to come.
She has skillfully
crafted poetry
since 1992
expanding into
spoken word
over ten years ago.
As a performer,
she has entertained
and mesmerized people
at a variety of private affairs,
public events, and open-mics.
As a writer,
you are savoring
the initial fruit
of her labor.

Enjoy!

SALES

contact me on social media

to find out about upcoming events:

facebook, twitter, instagram:

Curv Brown

to obtain more of my works,

visit my website:

CurvBrown.com

thank you for purchasing my products

SHOWS

for booking,

contact me with your details via

CurvBrown.com

serious inquiries only